Asynchronous Programming in Python

Apply asyncio in Python to build scalable, high-performance apps across multiple scenarios

Nicolas Bohorquez

‹packt›

Asynchronous Programming in Python

Portfolio Director: Kunal Chaudhari

Relationship Lead: Samriddhi Murarka

Project Manager: K. Loganathan

Content Engineer: Alexander Powell

Technical Editor: Sumant Jadhav

Copy Editor: Alexander Powell

Indexer: Pratik Shirodkar

Proofreader: Alexander Powell

Production Designer: Ganesh Bhadwalkar

Growth Lead: Vinishka Kalra

First published: November 2025

Production reference: 1201125

Published by Packt Publishing Ltd.

Grosvenor House

11 St Paul's Square

Birmingham

B3 1RB, UK

ISBN 978-1-83664-661-7

www.packtpub.com

To my father, Jose Bohorquez, and my mother, Myriam Gutierrez, for their sacrifices and their determination to demonstrate that education is the key to development. To my wife W for being my loving partner throughout our non-stop adventure. To my son Matias, for giving me back the joy of innocence.

— Nicolas Bohorquez

Contributors

About the author

Nicolas Bohorquez is founder and director of NBCS, a software consulting firm, with a focus on the intersection of augmented intelligence and software architecture, working on a variety of projects ranging from digitalization of business processes through automation and artificial intelligence to cloud costs control mechanisms. Prior to this, Nicolas has worked as lead architect and data architect at several startups in the Americas, focused on designing and developing data ingestion and processing systems, and combining his passion for writing historical fiction novels.

I want to thank the people who have been close to me and supported me, especially my wife W and my son Matias. I want to extend my gratitude to all my classmates and teachers who helped me become a passionate Systems Engineer. Finally, many thanks to the companies that challenged me to find solutions for problems that once seemed to be complex.

About the reviewers

Jed Horne has had a 20-year tech career in Silicon Valley and Latin America, primarily as a Python and Golang developer before switching to leading technology teams at US and international startups. He grew up in New Orleans, Louisiana, went to school at MIT and UC Berkeley, and currently lives in Bogotá, Colombia. He has a particular interest in backend technologies for mapping applications and worked on the first version of Apple Maps before taking a role at Uber where he worked from 2013–2018. Currently, he works with Nicolás at a construction-tech company called Source based in Portland, OR. He is really good at Ms. Pacman, and hopes his children will follow in his footsteps.

Niels Freier is a technology leader and software architect with a passion for crafting elegant and innovative solutions in software and data systems. He founded his own cybersecurity startup before joining the Boston Consulting Group as a Principal AI Engineer, where he helped global organizations harness AI and data engineering at scale. Niels now works with British Airways, driving the modernization of enterprise data platforms with a focus on performance, scalability, and architectural excellence.

Table of Contents

Preface

Python is a versatile and popular programming language. Its adoption has been underpinned by the community-led development of a large number of powerful and well-documented libraries, with the result that it is now widely used across a variety of domains including data science, data engineering, scientific computing, artificial intelligence and more.

In many application domains, the scalability and performance of Python-based solutions can be significantly boosted by applying asynchronous programming techniques – so much so that it could be argued that asynchronous programming is now essential for modern Python development. By allowing multiple operations to run simultaneously it can dramatically reduce execution time, especially for I/O-bound tasks, enabling solutions to handle increasing demands efficiently.

Nevertheless, not all workloads lend themselves to processing by asynchronous methods; for some tasks performance penalties may be incurred, or solutions just become more complicated than necessary. The effective application of asynchronous programming techniques therefore requires the developer to possess a secure understanding of the basic underlying concepts, and knowledge of how constraints on the application of asynchronous approaches come about. The aim of this book is to give you, the reader, that knowledge and understanding, so that you can make effective use of the power of asynchronous programming in your own projects.

The book effectively consists of two blocks of chapters. In *Chapters 1 to 6* we look at asynchronous programming fundamentals and core mechanisms like `asyncio` and `Trio`, and also consider various pitfalls and their avoidance, and how to measure and test our asynchronous solutions. Then in *Chapters 7 to 10* asynchronous techniques are applied to real-world scenarios involving web frameworks, databases, data pipelines, and simulations.

Who this book is for

Developers, data scientists, vibe coders and anyone else who uses Python regularly will gain practical insights into how to apply asynchronous programming mechanisms and patterns from this book.

- Python developers: you will learn how asynchronous programming patterns can improve decisions about implementations, so that they scale better and you avoid the common errors that lead to poor results when asynchronous programming is misused.
- Data scientists: you will gain an overview of how data-related operations can benefit from the application of asynchronous programming constructs such as generators and coroutines.
- Vibe coders: when boilerplate code generation is carried out by a specialized large language model (LLM), this book will help you read and maybe improve some of the implementation details of the alternatives offered by the model.

What this book covers

Chapter 1 contrasts synchronous and asynchronous programming, highlighting the latter's potential to reduce execution time. It defines OS processes and threads, then explains some of the important Python abstractions, such as green threads, fibers, and coroutines for cooperative multitasking.

Chapter 2 focuses on how asynchronous programming maximizes hardware efficiency. It distinguishes concurrency from parallelism, and then demonstrates these principles using Python's multiprocessing and multithreading capabilities, emphasizing thread safety with synchronization primitives.

Chapter 3 introduces generators as specialized iterators and defines the concept of coroutines, before exploring how to pass arguments to those coroutines. The chapter then covers the application of some of Python's benchmarking tools for measuring CPU and wall time.

Chapter 4 explores `asyncio` as Python's standard mechanism for asynchronous tasks, defining awaitables as the core concept behind the implementation. It stresses non-blocking tasks for efficiency and presents ways of integrating synchronous code. The chapter also introduces `Trio` as an alternative, highlighting its structured concurrency model.

Chapter 5 details common errors in asynchronous programming that hinder scaling. It introduces a more comprehensive tool for profiling CPU and I/O usage, and then we elaborate on key mistakes commonly found in asynchronous implementations. The chapter also covers improved exception handling and non-blocking logging as complementary techniques to prevent I/O bottlenecks.

Chapter 6 explores asynchronous design patterns. It covers testing of asynchronous implementations using standard tools. Some common patterns for solving asynchronous-favorable use cases, like the half-sync/half-async pattern, monitor object pattern and the read-write lock pattern, are presented in detail.

Chapter 7 explores asynchronous programming in Python web frameworks. It reviews the MVC pattern and traces the evolution from synchronous implementations to true asynchronous processing that involves protocols like HTTP and WebSockets.

Chapter 8 focuses on optimizing asynchronous data access, especially relational database engines, including embedded and external options. The chapter also evaluates object-relational mappers, weighing their benefits against potential architectural coupling and performance issues.

Chapter 9 explores building efficient asynchronous data pipelines for ETL/ELT operations, utilizing the Pipes and Filters pattern. It demonstrates how you can orchestrate asynchronous steps for I/O-bound tasks using a multilingual etymology dataset example.

Chapter 10 explores asynchronous computing in interactive notebooks, using Agent Based Modeling (ABM) to simulate wealth inequality via the Boltzmann Wealth Model. The simulation delegates agent decisions to external LLMs via non-blocking HTTP requests, an I/O-bound scenario.

To get the most out of this book

You will need to understand the basics of the Python programming language, virtual environments, and the execution of docker containers to get the most of the code presented in this book.

Software/hardware covered in the book	Operating system requirements
Python 3.9	Linux, macOS or Windows
Docker or Podman	
Ollama or other local LLM execution environment	
Django 4.x	
Flask 3.x	
Quart 0.20	
Uvicorn 0.38	
Hypercorn 0.17	
Scalene 1.5	
Postgresql 17	
Gephi 0.9	

If you are using the digital version of this book, we advise you to type the code yourself or access the code from the book's GitHub repository (a link is available in the next section). Doing so will help you avoid any potential errors related to the copying and pasting of code.

Download the example code files

You can download the example code files for this book from GitHub at `https://github.com/PacktPublishing/Asynchronous-Programming-in-Python`. If there's an update to the code, it will be updated in the GitHub repository. We also have other code bundles from our rich catalog of books and videos available at `https://github.com/PacktPublishing/`. Check them out!

Code in Action

The Code in Action videos for this book can be viewed at `http://bit.ly/20QfDum`.

Download the color images

We also provide a PDF file that has color images of the screenshots and diagrams used in this book. You can download it here: http://packt.link/gbp/9781836646617.

Conventions used

There are a number of text conventions used throughout this book.

Code in text: Indicates code words in text, database table names, folder names, filenames, file extensions, pathnames, dummy URLs, user input, and Twitter handles. Here is an example: "Python's threading reading module is wrapped by the multiprocessing.dummy module to offer an API-level compatible Pool subclass (ThreadPool) that implements parallelization work by using threads instead of processes."

A block of code is set as follows:

```
class Author(Model):
    id = fields.IntField(pk=True)
    name = fields.CharField(max_length=255)
    books: fields.ReverseRelation["Book"]
    def __str__(self):
        return self.name
    class Meta:
        ordering = ["name"]
```

Any command-line input or output is written as follows:

```
$ python3 -m venv .env
$ source .env/bin/activate
$ pip install -r requirements.txt
```

Bold: Indicates a new term, an important word, or words that you see onscreen. For instance, words in menus or dialog boxes appear in **bold**. Here is an example: " CPython, includes a mechanism – known as the **global interpreter lock** or **GIL** – to ensure that there is only one thread executing Python code in a process."

> Warnings or important notes appear like this.

Tips and tricks appear like this.

Get in touch

Feedback from our readers is always welcome.

General feedback: If you have questions about any aspect of this book, email us at customercare@ packtpub.com and mention the book title in the subject of your message.

Errata: Although we have taken every care to ensure the accuracy of our content, mistakes do happen. If you have found a mistake in this book, we would be grateful if you would report this to us. Please visit www.packtpub.com/support/errata and fill in the form.

Piracy: If you come across any illegal copies of our works in any form on the internet, we would be grateful if you would provide us with the location address or website name. Please contact us at copyright@packt.com with a link to the material.

If you are interested in becoming an author: If there is a topic that you have expertise in and you are interested in either writing or contributing to a book, please visit authors.packtpub.com.

Share your thoughts

Once you've read *Asynchronous Programming in Python*, we'd love to hear your thoughts! Scan the QR code below to go straight to the Amazon review page for this book and share your feedback.

https://packt.link/r/1836646615

Your review is important to us and the tech community and will help us make sure we're delivering excellent quality content.

Free Benefits with Your Book

This book comes with free benefits to support your learning. Activate them now for instant access (see the *"How to Unlock"* section for instructions).

Here's a quick overview of what you can instantly unlock with your purchase:

PDF and ePub Copies   **Next-Gen Web-Based Reader**

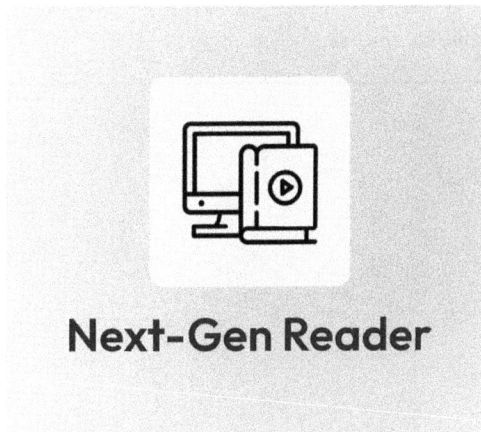

Free PDF and ePub versions   **Next-Gen Reader**

Access a DRM-free PDF copy of this book to read anywhere, on any device.

Use a DRM-free ePub version with your favorite e-reader.

Multi-device progress sync: Pick up where you left off, on any device.

Highlighting and notetaking: Capture ideas and turn reading into lasting knowledge.

Bookmarking: Save and revisit key sections whenever you need them.

Dark mode: Reduce eye strain by switching to dark or sepia themes.

How to Unlock

UNLOCK NOW

Scan the QR code (or go to packtpub.com/unlock). Search for this book by name, confirm the edition, and then follow the steps on the page.

Note: *Keep your invoice handy. Purchases made directly from Packt don't require one.*

1

Synchronous and Asynchronous Programming Paradigms

An algorithm is defined broadly in the Merrian-Webster Dictionary as a 'step-by-step procedure for solving a problem or accomplishing some end'. Step-by-step is commonly understood to imply that the steps are executed sequentially, that is to say, step 0 at time instant 0 and step 1 at time instant 1, etc.

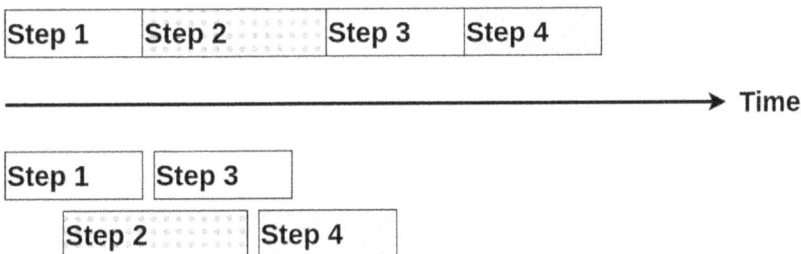

Asynchronous programming is very difficult to grasp because it introduces the idea that there could be more than one line of execution running at the same time, which means you might have situations in which step n and step $n+1$ of your algorithm are executed at the very same instant t. The following image presents an approximation of both synchronous and asynchronous models. Note the performance gain obtained by implementing an asynchronous solution:

Synchronous

| Step 1 | Step 2 | Step 3 | Step 4 |

⟶ **Time**

| Step 1 | Step 3 |

| Step 2 | Step 4 |

Asynchronous

Figure 1.1: An oversimplified timeline comparison between synchronous and asynchronous solutions

The consequences of this are huge: with the right design, algorithms can be executed in dramatically less time, freeing up resources and mental energy for programmers and companies alike.

Asynchronous programming poses a number of challenges that must be understood if we are to unlock the full potential of these new algorithms. (*How do you split the tasks you want to execute in parallel? What happens if one task ends before another? Who coordinates the tasks? Etc.*) That's why we start this book with a discussion of the core concepts that a developer must understand to get started:

- Synchronous and asynchronous programming
- Operating system process and threads
- Green threads, coroutines and fibers
- Callbacks, promises and futures
- Challenges of asynchronous programming

Free Benefits with Your Book

Your purchase includes a free PDF copy of this book along with other exclusive benefits. Check the *Free Benefits with Your Book* section in the Preface to unlock them instantly and maximize your learning experience.

Technical requirements

Sample code provided in this chapter is available on Github (`https://github.com/PacktPublishing/Asynchronous-Programming-in-Python/tree/main/Chapter01`). You don't need anything special installed on your computer besides Python 3; if you need help with installation check the community instructions at `https://wiki.python.org/moin/BeginnersGuide`.

Understanding synchronous and asynchronous programming

As in many aspects of life, programming requires clear objectives if success is to be achieved, and those objectives are usually formulated as objectively testable requirements. A set of requirements represents all the characteristics that a software solution must exhibit to be deemed satisfactory, i.e. the things that you must check to accept or reject a solution. They can include functional and non-functional aspects. Functional aspects are directly related to the product definition ('If I do X, Y happens') whereas **non-functional requirements** are not directly related to the solution per se but may be required for other reasons (e.g. 'Implement using the Cloud to guarantee a certain level of availability').

For example, in sports or board games there is usually the clear objective of winning a match, and it is usually easy to evaluate whether the player has achieved that objective or not. In basketball, you can see if the ball has passed through the hoop. The shot clock is an example of a non-functional requirement: it's not necessary for scoring but is an important rule of the game nonetheless that must be complied with to avoid a penalty.

Synchronous programming: chess

A good way to learn how to think in a synchronous and structured way is to solve little chess puzzles. Chess is a 'complete information' game, which means that everybody involved in a game has complete awareness of the situation of the game. A chess puzzle is an individual practice mode in which the player must find a solution for an established game situation to finish the game (checkmate). Usually, chess puzzles have an optimal solution which is defined as the solution requiring the fewest moves to reach checkmate.

> **Important note**
>
> If you don't know the rules of chess, a good introduction is available from the libre/ free community-driven server located at https://lichess.org/learn.

The following chess puzzle can be optimally solved by the white player in three moves:

Figure 1.2: A chess puzzle solvable in three moves by white

To solve this kind of problem the player must make their moves sequentially, taking into account the global state of the game (the positions of the pieces on the board), the value of each piece (for in chess each available piece type has a different value), and the potential reactions the opponent may make to the player's moves. Remember that chess is a turn-based strategy game.

Many problems can be solved in this way, which we refer to as **synchronous programming** – the decomposition of steps into a cascade having a single line or thread of control. The execution of each step and time of execution are perfectly synchronized, and each step has full information about the global status, variables and available resources.

The following table shows the solution of the previous puzzle in three moves for white. Notice that the flow might change if conditions varied with the opponent's moves (for example if in Step 1(b) the black player made a mistake):

Step	White (a)	Black (b)
1	Bh8	Nd4
2	Qd4	Be6
3	Qg7	

Table 1.1: Solution for the chess puzzle

Asynchronous programming: soccer

A game like soccer is much more complex than chess. It involves two teams composed of 11 players each, and players are assigned positions (goalkeeper, defender, midfielder, forward) which impact their initial locations and potentially their ability to perform certain actions. The overall objective is to score (cause the ball to cross the opponent's goal line). Any player can do this, and although at any given moment one team is defending and the other is attacking, the roles are fluid and continuous and 'turns' at shooting to goal are often unexpected.

The nature of the game allows for an infinite number of strategies. Usually, a team's strategy involves not only retaining the ball but also making teammates run to distract the opposing team and to gradually occupy favorable 'real estate' on the field to improve the chances of any given shot.

The following three diagrams show a typical soccer play in which a defender takes control of the ball and after three moves scores a goal:

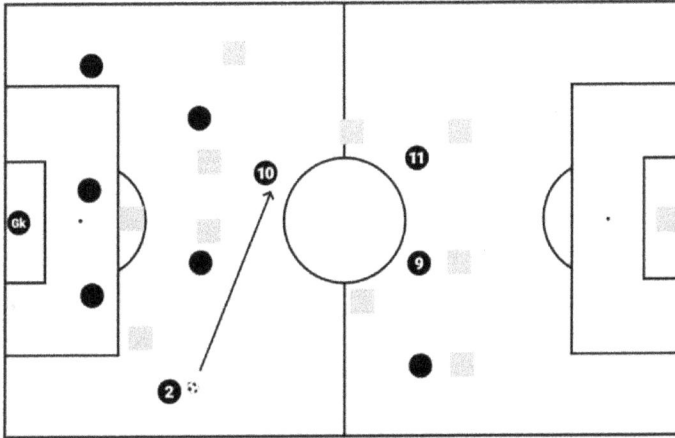

Figure 1.3: A soccer play starts with number 2 making a pass to number 10

The main execution timeline is always the one in which the ball is involved. Here it starts with player 2 taking control of the ball and making a pass to player 10, but once the pass is executed player 2 starts to run to a new position.

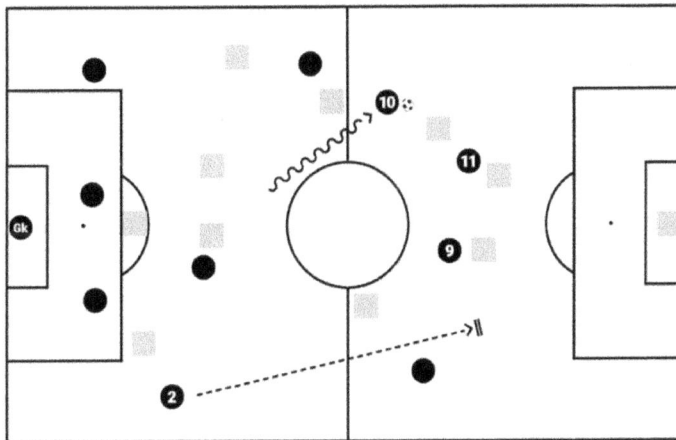

Figure 1.4: Second move: a dribble by number 10 and a run by number 2

At the second instant in time, multiple things are happening: player 10 dribbles past an opponent, while players 9, 2, and 11 move downfield for better positioning.

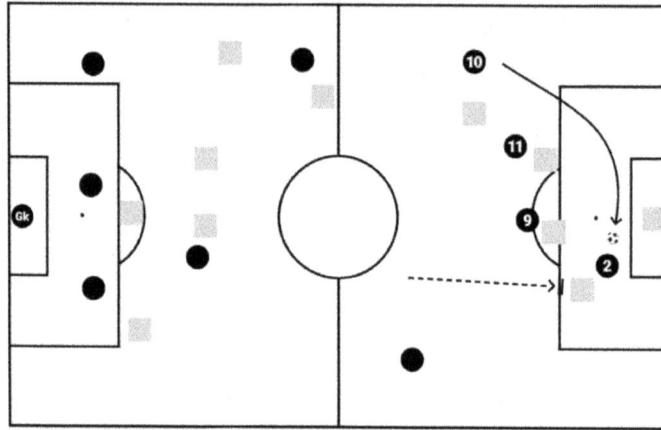

Figure 1.5: Third move: number 2 scores

At the third instant, player 10 waits until player 2 is in position to score, after which he passes the ball and player 2 is able to hit the net. The main execution line (scoring the goal) cannot be achieved if the supporting, parallel executions by multiple players are not completed.

> **Note**
>
> The previous example is an adaptation of a real play executed by the Slovenian national soccer team in the 2024 UEFA European Football Championship, the match report for which is available at `https://www.uefa.com`.

In the same way, asynchronous programming is a technique in which some of an algorithm's steps are executed in different lines of control than the main one, and those executions may occur simultaneously. **Simultaneous execution** is usually managed by the operating system or the programming language runtime, but simultaneous execution is not a requirement for asynchronous programming: asynchronous operations can also be run sequentially if desired.

It's important to note that the multiple control lines in asynchronous programming don't block each other. As in soccer, individual operations (the equivalent of players in soccer) are free to run unimpeded as other actions occur around them.

We have used the idea of *control line* in both examples without a formal definition. This is because there are several ways that modern computers control the execution of programs, depending on hardware characteristics, scheduling algorithms, memory management, and I/O handling. Moreover, programming languages and frameworks have their own approaches to concurrency that may vary depending on OS or hardware constraints.

In this section, we have introduced three key concepts which will be developed throughout the book: synchronous solutions, asynchronous solutions, and lines of control. Those concepts will be further elaborated in the specific context of computer science in the following section, to help you move from intuition and sports metaphors to real computer programming.

Operating system process and threads

Central Processing Units (CPUs) function in a fetch – execute cycle. Specifically, the operating system (OS) fetches a set of instructions (program) from disk into memory, and they are then executed by the CPU. A program being executed is called a **process**. Loading a program into memory to become a process implies dividing memory into these sections:

- **Text**: This section of the memory allocated typically contains compiled code with a static set of instructions

- **Data:** Static data and global variables required for a running process

- **Heap**: Space reserved for dynamically allocated data structures (non-static, non-global variables)

- **Stack:** Local variables used in functions, which, if large enough, can compete with allocated heap space (causing a 'stack overflow' or 'insufficient heap space' error)

Although in an asynchronous program it may appear that all instructions in the set are being called at exactly the same time, technically each step is broken into blocks which are scheduled to be executed by the OS. Those blocks are executed so fast that it gives the impression that a processor is computing several things at the same time.

The change from execution of code blocks from one process to execution of blocks from another is a costly operation, called **context switching**. Context switching involves managing interruptions in the processing of a block, knowing the execution status of any given process, and waiting for other processes to complete, among other requirements for proper process flow.

Introducing threads

Modern computers typically have **multiple cores**, each of which is capable of executing a process. To better handle context switching, an abstraction was created: a **thread**, or atomic unit of processing. Each thread runs on a single core, and a processor can simultaneously run multiple threads from a single process by taking advantage of this architecture.

Threads are also called lightweight processes, since they must each individually conform to the structure described above for processes, but there is an important consideration: multiple threads of a process share the memory heap and code/data segments, which means that programmers must be careful to ensure that shared resource constraints are adhered to, but each thread maintains its own private stack.

The following diagram shows how processing can vary according to CPU and OS characteristics:

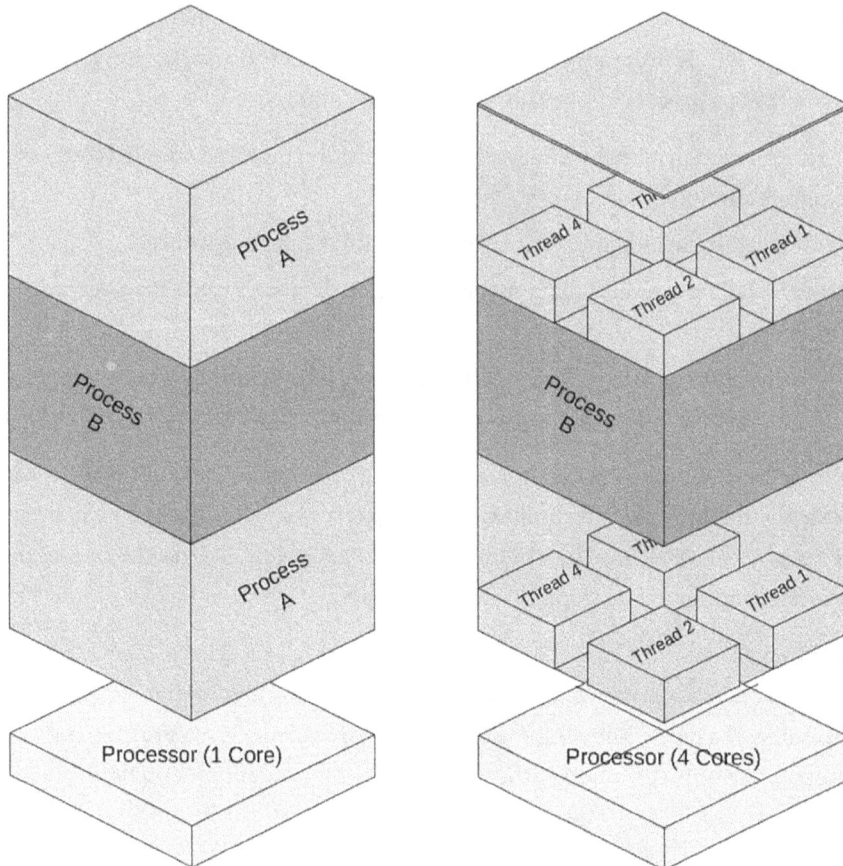

Figure 1.6: A single process/single thread processor on the left and a multithreaded processor on the right

What happens if a process has more threads than available cores? Thread context switching is *'lighter'* because it involves saving and restoring less state, while process context switching is *'heavier'* because it involves saving and restoring more state, including memory mappings. Therefore, in terms of efficiency, context switching between threads is generally faster and less resource-intensive than context switching between processes.

Some pieces of software are multiprocessor but not multithreaded, meaning that all processes are single-threaded (synchronous) but they can be split to take advantage of multiple processors.

There are two types of thread: **kernel threads** and **user threads**. User threads are created, managed, and bounded via the **Application Programming Interface (API)** provided by a system's OS and managed by the individual program being run. The key point about user threads is that if one of them performs blocking operations, the entire process is blocked. This impacts the way multithreaded programs are designed.

The lifecycle of kernel threads, on the other hand, is entirely managed by the operating system. This type of thread has the advantage that if an operation blocks thread execution, the parent process is not blocked. Python's default threading model is managed by the underlying operating system kernel, even if by default only one thread can run the interpreter at the time. We will explore this design in more detail in *Chapter 2*.

Processes, kernel threads and user threads are constructs that involve close management of the physical resources of a computer. As you might expect, modern programming languages provide abstractions to efficiently manage these concepts and the underlying resources. In the next section we will discuss three programming concepts central to **multitasking**: green threads, coroutines and fibers.

Green threads, coroutines and fibers

Just as user threads are overlaid on kernel threads via the OS API, **green threads** are implemented entirely within the runtime or virtual machine provided by the programming language. In Python, scheduling responsibility for green threads is part of the interpreter process that runs the threads.

The following table summarizes the most important differences between Python's native threads and green threads:

Aspect	Threads	Green threads
Execution control	Implemented via native operating system kernel, which means that a thread's execution can be interrupted by the operating system at any time even when it is in the middle of an operation.	Each thread runs until the scheduler interrupts its operation; scheduling mechanisms are implemented by the programming language.
Portability	Depends on the threading model implemented by the operating system, which means that race conditions and memory allocation depend on the OS rather than the program.	Given that the implementation of the scheduler and thread model is native to the programming language, you can expect more consistent behavior across different runtime environments.
Resource utilization	Each thread has its own stack of resources, sharing memory allocated by the parent process.	Runtime environment allocates isolated memory spaces per thread.
Multi-processing	Generally prevented by the global interpreter (CPython), but workarounds are possible.	Not possible, as threads are bound by the master running process.

Table 1.2: Characteristics of threads and green threads

Many programming languages have implemented green threads as their primary multitasking solution, but due to the limitations for multi-processing most have evolved to allow for cooperative multitasking through fibers and coroutines.

Fibers and coroutines

Fibers are like green threads in that they use a runtime scheduler that is independent of the underlying OS. However, instead of running until the scheduler interrupts their execution, fibers cooperate by ceding control to the next fiber in the same process. (Think of yarn being composed of multiple individual threads woven together.) This is also called **cooperative multitasking**.

A common drawback of fibers is that because scheduling control is passed to the developer, some fibers run or utilize resources over an extended period, reducing the resources available for execution of other fibers. Usually, fibers run inside a single thread.

The next step in the evolution of asynchronous processing is the **coroutine**, which is a function that can pause its own execution and later be resumed at the point at which it was interrupted. The following code starts the execution of a coroutine, then pauses its execution until some data is passed to resume the operation:

```
import datetime
def date_coroutine(_date:datetime.datetime):
    print(f"Your appointment is scheduled for {_date.strftime('%m/%d/%Y,
%H:%M:%S')}")
    while True:
        current_date = (yield)
        if current_date > _date:
            print("Oops, your appointment already passed")
        else:
            print("You have time")

d1 = datetime.datetime(1981, 6, 29, 1, 0)
coroutine = date_coroutine(d1)
coroutine.__next__()
d2 = datetime.datetime(2018, 5, 3)
coroutine.send(d2)
```

The date_coroutine is initialized with d1, but it's not executed until the __next__() method is invoked. It starts by printing the value of the argument, then waits until data is passed via the send() method. Notice that there are two points of access to the method, and run time may vary. Coroutines will be explored deeply in *Chapter 3*.

Multitasking features are a two-way street – you need to communicate with them to understand whether they have been executed if you want to trigger another dependent process. Callbacks, futures, and promises are ways to manage these flows.

Callbacks, futures and promises

Callbacks are functions that are passed as arguments to other functions or functions that are called inside other functions. These functions can be invoked when an event occurs. Callbacks are usually used as a join point for **multithreading/multiprocessing** solutions. The following example shows a toy example of a callback function that is invoked from each thread, after the thread has done some processing:

```python
def worker(num, callback):
    print(f"Worker {num} starting...")
    time.sleep(num)  # Simulate some work
    print(f"Worker {num} finished.")
    callback(num)  # Call the callback

def callback_function(num):
    print(f"Callback for worker {num} called.")

if __name__ == "__main__":
    threads = []
    for i in range(5):
        thread = threading.Thread(target=worker, args=(i, callback_function))
        threads.append(thread)
        thread.start()
    for thread in threads:
        thread.join()
```

Multiprocessing and multithreading callbacks are treated in detail in *Chapter 2*. While very popular some time ago in other languages, such as JavaScript, this mechanism has some drawbacks that need to be mitigated, including nesting of callbacks, difficult debugging and **race conditions**. Other mechanisms have been developed to address these and other difficulties, like **futures** and **promises**.

The result of an asynchronous call is unknown at the start of the main thread's execution, and the future/promise concept allows programmers to wait until something is returned before continuing a process. Futures/promises can be awaited up until their execution finishes and can execute a callback function when they end.

Semantics for futures/promises vary by programming language. In Python, futures are part of the standard language API, but promises are implemented by the community based on the Promises/ A+ (`https://promisesaplus.com/implementations`) specification. Futures and promises are covered in detail in *Chapter 4*.

Challenges of asynchronous programming

Besides the many concepts explored in this chapter, probably the three most important challenges that a programmer faces when designing an asynchronous solution are:

- **Setting expectations**: not all programming constructs are applicable in all contexts, and they come with costs. CPU- and I/O-bounded problems may not always benefit from multi-threaded approaches.

- **Testing/debugging asynchronous code**: testing is a crucial aspect of modern programming, and threads and coroutines can be complicated to debug. Some techniques and common patterns have been developed, and they will be discussed in later sections.

- **Thread safety**: shared resources always impose access management challenges. Concurrent changes to stored data are an obvious challenge, so it's important to keep in mind key concepts like ACID compliance when designing database solutions. Likewise, shared resources (volatile/non-volatile memory, callback execution) must guarantee execution safety in multi-thread environments.

Summary

In this chapter we have informally introduced several key terms and concepts. In the next chapter we will go deep into actual Python constructs for multiprocessing and multithreading, including problems in which those techniques bring more value.

We learned in an intuitive way how to distinguish synchronous and asynchronous solutions to well-defined problems. Then we translated those ideas into standard computer science terminology. This will allow us to go deeper into the particulars of each concept as we focus on specific coding solutions. In *Chapter 2* we will embark on the practical approach by coding and comparing the multiprocessing and multithreading solutions for a vanilla implementation of a CPU-intensive problem.

Get This Book's PDF Version and Exclusive Extras

UNLOCK NOW

Scan the QR code (or go to packtpub.com/unlock). Search for this book by name, confirm the edition, and then follow the steps on the page.

Note: Keep your invoice handy. Purchases made directly from Packt don't require one.

2

Identifying Concurrency and Parallelism

In his famous 1995 article '*A Plea for Lean Software*' (`https://www.computer.org/csdl/magazine/co/1995/02/r2064/13rRUwInv7E`), Turing Award-winner Niklaus Wirth postulated that '*software is getting slower more rapidly than hardware is becoming faster*'. The adage encapsulates the state of the software industry at nearly any point in time, and is still relevant today. As a data point, it is worth reading NASA's contractor report about the computer systems used in actual spaceflight or in close support of it (`https://ntrs.nasa.gov/api/citations/19880069935/downloads/19880069935_Optimized.pdf`). Given the hardware resources we have now, and contrasting them with the very limited hardware available decades ago, current capabilities and performance look abysmal. Why do we have slower systems if there has been an incredible increase in hardware capability over recent decades? How can we get our software to use more efficiently the hardware resources available?

My conjecture is that trends in the emergence of complexity in systems (`https://en.wikipedia.org/wiki/Complex_system`) are implicated, but in this chapter we are going to explore the most common suggestion to improve solutions that are *too slow*. We are going to introduce the concepts of **concurrency** and **parallelism** in an abstract way before tackling a problem that can be solved via several approaches, applying Python's multiprocessing and multithreading capabilities to increasing degrees. Then we will present a method for measuring the performance gains obtained by applying the previously presented techniques. Finally, we shall discuss some heuristics for detecting problems that are good candidates for parallel processing, better known as *embarrassingly parallel workloads*.

The concurrency and parallelism concepts, along with the ability to detect problems for which Python's tooling would be a good fit, will help you to discard the techniques in scenarios where the likely gains are insufficient to cover the additional complexity or overhead of implementing a multiprocessing solution.

To summarize, in this chapter we're going to cover the following main topics:

- Understanding concurrency and parallelism
- Applying multiprocessing and multithreading
- Detecting embarrassingly parallel workloads

Technical requirements

In this chapter we will show different solutions to a common problem. To run the code, which is available in the *Chapter02* folder of the Github repo at https://github.com/PacktPublishing/ Asynchronous-Programming-in-Python, we recommend creating a new virtual environment inside the folder and then running each Python file to check its output. No external packages are required but this way you can isolate your execution from the common Python environment of your computer:

```
$ python3 -m venv .env
$ source .env/bin/activate
```

Understanding concurrency and parallelism

Concurrency refers to the number of simultaneous tasks a system executes. Computers' processors execute atomic operations at amazing speed, but they execute them one at a time. The result is that it looks like they are executing non-atomic tasks simultaneously.

To illustrate the idea, the following diagram shows two programs, each of which consists of three atomic operations: a processing task, reading a long file, and finally, another processing task:

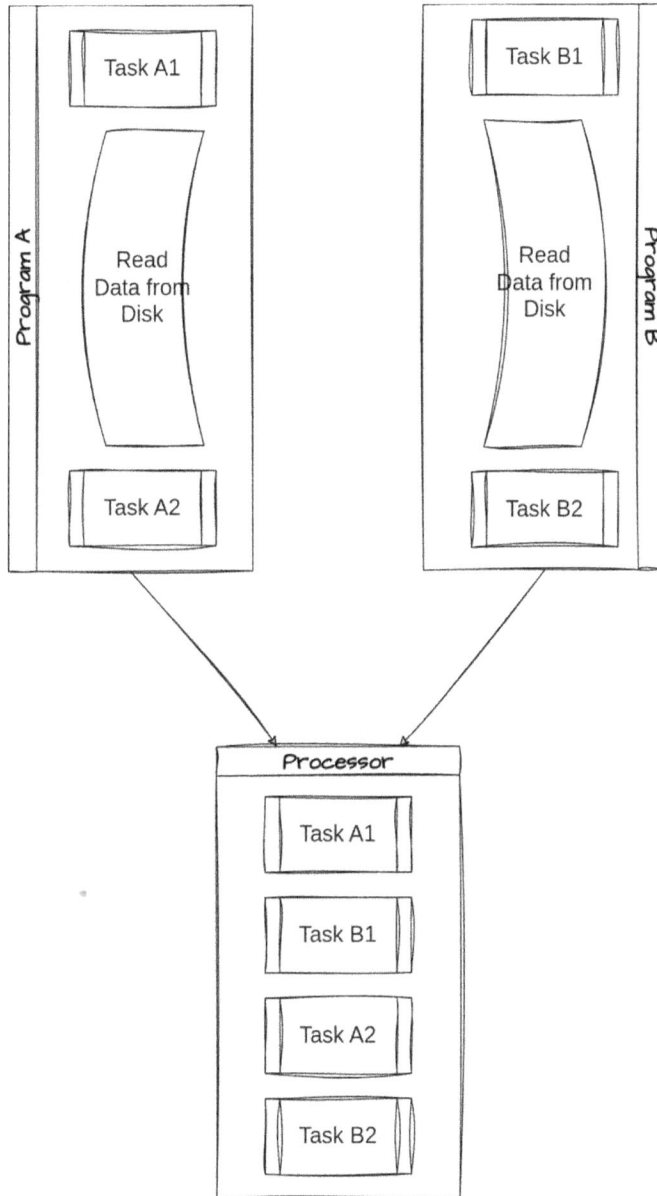

Figure 2.1: Two concurrent programs being executed by a single processor

Imagine that both programs are launched at the same time. The processor executes the first atomic task of one of them and when there is a blocking operation that depends on a resource other than the processing unit, it uses the interruption mechanism to execute the first task of the second program. Both programs are executed concurrently by the processor.

Python offers several mechanisms to handle concurrency in a program: threads, coroutines, and asynchronous programming features. However, when you have several processors, the execution of programs and their atomic operations can be completely separated and handled by different processors. In this case, we are talking about **parallel processing**.

To illustrate parallelism, the following diagram shows a computer with six processors (P1 to P6) that must handle 10 programs (W1 to W10) simultaneously. At the start each of the first six programs is assigned to a processor, and once one of them is free one of the remaining programs will be assigned for execution.

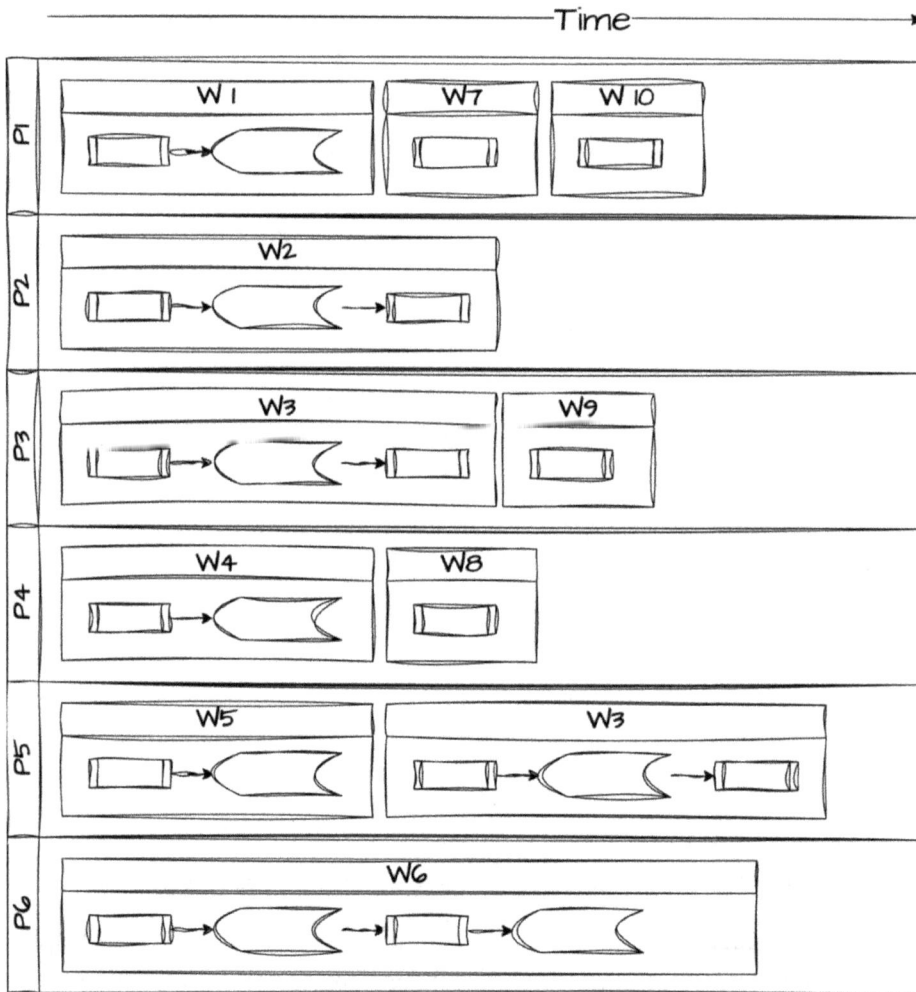

Figure 2.2: Several workloads executed in parallel

It's important to note that the additional resources are not required to be on the same machine; you can distribute a workload between several processing units of different computers.

In cloud computing, there is the concept of **Function as a Service (FaaS)**, in which cloud providers offer an isolated execution environment (with some restrictions on execution time and computational resources) for small functions, and as the load increases so the number of environments is automatically increased. Therefore, in cloud computing, FaaS handles concurrency by using parallelism in its execution.

Concurrency and parallelism are better understood in practical situations. The next section will examine a vanilla implementation of a solution against a simple multiprocessing implementation and a multithreading one. Later this will open the door to a discussion of thread safety as a non-functional requirement.

Applying multiprocessing and multithreading

Applying multiprocessing or multithreading techniques to any code isn't a good choice; concurrency and parallelism are best reserved for the problem spaces where they provide the best results. As a rule of thumb, if a problem is input- or output-bound, it is better suited to being solved by increasing the concurrency handling of the system. If the problem requires more processing than data management, it is CPU-bound, and then multiprocessing is the best approach.

Usually, however, it is not that simple. Distributed systems, with their reliance on network communication, inherently have I/O characteristics that make them more suitable for the application of concurrency management techniques, while some of the components of the distributed systems could use the power of local/distributed processors to accelerate execution (e.g. when a specific large task is distributed across multiple parallel processors with a framework like MapReduce).

Extract, transform and load (ETL) use cases are good examples of problems in which concurrency and multiprocessing can be combined. Extraction and load tasks usually make heavy use of network resources, but transformations are usually applied in local data stores that could use the power of several CPUs. That's the theory; now we will explore how to apply those concepts and theories to a specific use case.

Sample case: finding flight distances

To analyze a problem in which multiprocessing/multithreading are suitable solutions, we'll present a scenario involving both I/O tasks and processing tasks. To apply the concepts previously discussed, we are going to implement a solution for a simple problem: calculating the distance between a set of cities.

Imagine that you are planning a trip without modern map apps and want to know the total mileage of your journey. The program should get a **comma-separated values (CSV)** file containing the coordinates of possible cities and a list of cities that will be visited. We are going to assume that cities will be visited in the order in which they are input.

The following diagram shows the flow of a possible solution. It starts by loading, line by line, each record of the cities CSV file. Then the list of cities is regrouped into a list of tuples (source city, destination city). After that, we need to calculate the distance between each tuple to finally calculate the total aggregated distance.

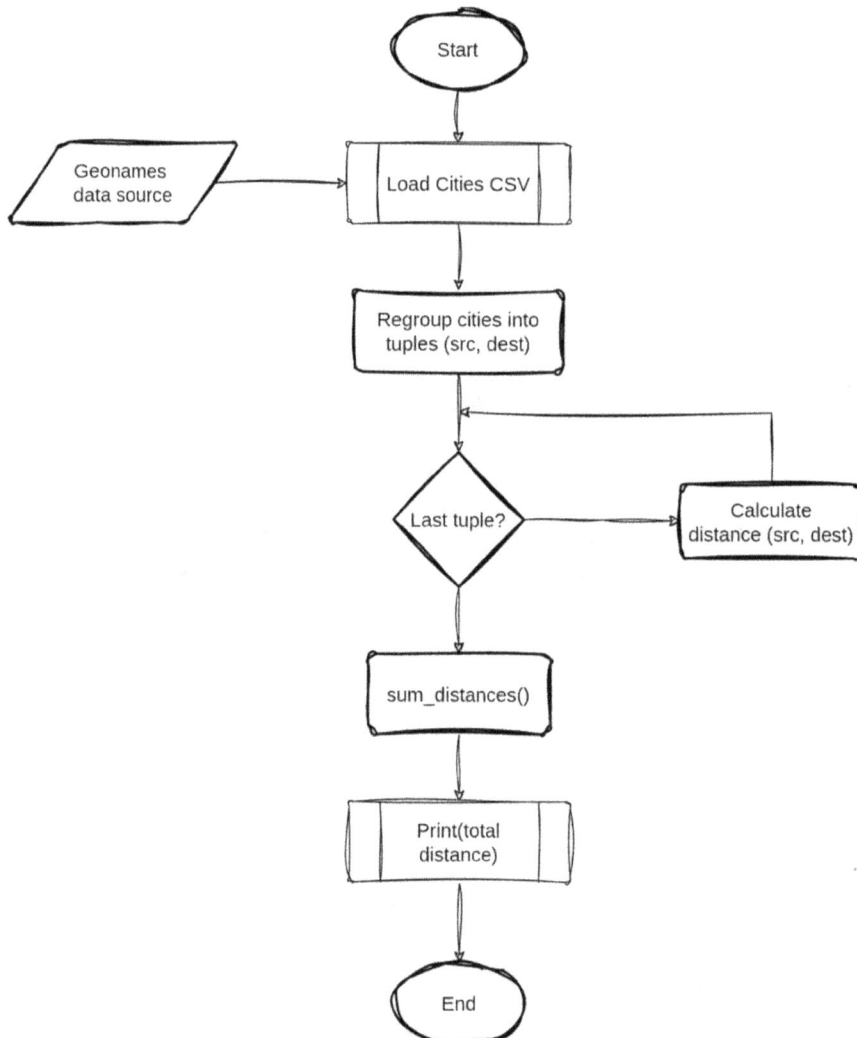

Figure 2.3: A flow diagram for a distance calculator program

There are several ways to calculate distances. A simple way to think about it is to use two points [(x1,y1), (x2,y2)] in a Cartesian plane and apply the Euclidean distance formula:

$distance = square\ root((x2 - x1)^2 + (y2 - y1)^2)$

But this approximation has a problem: the Earth is spherical. So for the sake of precision we are going to use the great-circle distance to get a better result. The details of the formulation are discussed in depth in the Aviation Formulary by Ed Williams (`http://www.edwilliams.org/avform147.htm#GCF`). The actual formula is:

$$distance = 2 * asin\left(sqrt\left(\left(sin((lat1 - lat2)/2)\right)^2 + cos(lat1) * cos(lat2) * \left(sin((lon1 - lon2)/2)\right)^2\right)\right)$$

In this formula, the `lat1` and `lat2` variables correspond to the latitude (`https://en.wikipedia.org/wiki/Latitude`) and `lon1` and `lon2` correspond to the longitude (`https://en.wikipedia.org/wiki/Longitude`) of the points on the earth's surface between which we are calculating the distance. Fortunately, the Simplemaps geographical database (`https://simplemaps.com/data/world-cities`) covers thousands of cities around the world, expressed in tuples with latitude and longitude coordinates, for free under the Creative Commons Attribution 4.0 license.

Now that we have established the theory, we can focus on implementing different solutions using the single-process, multi-process and multi-threaded approaches.

Important note

In Python, a global variable is a variable declared outside of any function or class, making it accessible from anywhere within the script. This means its value can be read by any part of the program. To *modify* a global variable within a function, however, use the `global` keyword to make it clear that you are referring to the global variable rather than creating a new local one with the same name. While global variables offer broad accessibility, their overuse can make code harder to understand and maintain due to potential side effects.

Where the following code examples use global variables, they do so for demonstration purposes only, in order to illustrate the desired behavior.

Single-process solution

The first solution attempt is a simple one. The code does exactly what is depicted in the previous diagram – it takes a CSV file and loads it into memory as a list of dictionaries using Python's csv module. Then, it parses the arguments to build the cities_to_be_visited list with tuples of (source_city, destination_city). After that, it iterates over the cities_to_be_visited list to calculate each tuple distance using the great_circle_distance function, and finally returns a total distance calculation:

```python
def cities_into_tuples(cities:List)->List:
    cities_list = []
    total_cities = len(cities)
    for i in range(0, total_cities):
        if i+1 < total_cities:
            cities_list.append((cities[i], cities[i+1],))
    return cities_list

def great_circle_distance(src_dest: Tuple)->Number:
    source = src_dest[0]
    dest = src_dest[1]
    lat1 = abs(float(source['lat'])*pi/180)
    lat2 = abs(float(dest['lat'])*pi/180)
    lon1 = abs(float(source['lng'])*pi/180)
    lon2 = abs(float(dest['lng'])*pi/180)
    distance = 2*asin(sqrt((sin((lat1-lat2)/2))**2 +
cos(lat1)*cos(lat2)*(sin((lon1-lon2)/2))**2))
    distance = distance*180*60/pi
    return distance
def calculate_path_distance(cities: List)->Number:
    total = 0
    for t in cities:
        d = great_circle_distance(t)
        print(f'From: {t[0]['city_ascii']} to: {t[1]['city_ascii']},
distance: {d} nm')
        total = total + d
    return total
```

In the source code available in the GitHub repository you can also find a couple of unit tests to validate the previous functions. You can run the code with a list of cities like this:

```
$ (.env) python -m test.test_solution1
$ (.env) python solution1.py Brasilia Tokyo "Guatemala City" Bogota Turin
Barcelona London "El Cairo" Casablanca "New York" "Los Angeles"
```

Make sure to use the double quotes for cities wich have more than one word in their names. You will get a series of '*From:x to:y, distance:z*' messages, along with the total distance. Now we have a baseline solution, which we can improve by taking advantage of the multitasking tools that Python offers. The first approach will be to modify the great_circle_distance function using multiprocessing, as shown in the next section.

Multiprocess solution

The canonical implementation of the Python programming language, CPython, includes a mechanism – known as the **global interpreter lock** or **GIL** – to ensure that there is only one thread executing Python code in a process. This decision has implications for performance in single- and multi-process systems, given that this implementation privileges the safety of access to some data types, such as *dictionaries*, and multi-threaded parallel programming over multiprocessing.

Besides that, the standard Python API also includes the multiprocessing module, which side-steps the GIL, allowing you to take advantage of machines with several processors. The most common way to use the multiprocessing module is to acquire a pool of worker processes that handle the execution of a function across multiple input values. This is called data parallelism and is suitable for improving our code. The following code, which is available in the Chapter 2/ solution2.py file, only changes the way the great_circle_distance function is invoked. Instead of iterating over the list of cities, we spawn two worker processes and use the pool to process the cities list:

```python
def calculate_path_distance(cities: List)->Number:
    total = 0
    with Pool(2) as p:
        values = p.map(great_circle_distance, cities)
        total = sum(values)
    return total
```

Multiprocessing pools make it easy to get parallelism up and working quickly but leave some questions open, such as: How do you communicate processes? In our specific case, how do we print the intermediate calculation of the distance between *a* and *b*? Python provides two ways to solve this. The first is the *shared state technique*, which means that some data will be stored in shared memory positions and can be accessed from any child process. This technique is supported by the multiprocessing Value and Array objects, but is highly discouraged given the issues that can potentially arise when you don't manage shared access resources properly.

The recommended way to communicate processes is through the multiprocessing Queue implementation, which provides a First In, First Out (FIFO) queue that locks the I/O from concurrent process access, guaranteeing that messages written/read into the queue are safe from memory corruption or race conditions. The following code shows how a global queue is declared in the main function and the great_circle_distance function assumes the producer role by putting the partial distance calculations as messages in the queue. The calculate_path_distance function acts as a consumer by printing the calculations once the entire list of cities is processed:

```python
def great_circle_distance(src_dest: Tuple)->Number:
    global queue
    source = src_dest[0]
    dest = src_dest[1]
    lat1 = abs(float(source['lat'])*pi/180)
    lat2 = abs(float(dest['lat'])*pi/180)
    lon1 = abs(float(source['lng'])*pi/180)
    lon2 = abs(float(dest['lng'])*pi/180)
    distance = 2*asin(sqrt((sin((lat1-lat2)/2))**2 +
cos(lat1)*cos(lat2)*(sin((lon1-lon2)/2))**2))
    distance = distance*180*60/pi
    queue.put(f'From: {source['city_ascii']} to: {dest['city_ascii']},
distance: {distance} nm')
    return distance
 def calculate_path_distance(cities: List)->Number:
    total = 0
    with Pool(2) as p:
        values = p.map(great_circle_distance, cities)
        total = sum(values)

    for i in range(len(cities)):
        msg = queue.get()
```

```
        print(msg)
    return total


if __name__ == '__main__':
    global queue
    queue = Queue()
    cities = load_csv('worldcities.csv')
    candidate_cities = load_city_args(sys.argv, cities)
    cities_to_be_visited = cities_into_tuples(candidate_cities)
    total = calculate_path_distance(cities_to_be_visited)
    print(f'Total distance: {total}nm')
```

Notice that the messages are not printed in the same order as that in which the cities are visited. That's because we cannot guarantee that each worker process will finish its execution at the same time.

You can also use the `multiprocessing` module to spawn child processes individually according to your needs. The module provides utilities to control the execution and lifecycle. To communicate directly between two processes, you can also use a direct mechanism defined by the `multiprocessing` Pipe class, which creates a direct channel in which each process has a connection that represents both ends of the pipe. Connections created have methods to send objects and receive data from the pipe.

A third interesting feature of the `multiprocessing` module is `Manager`, which can share objects by using proxy classes in a server process that can also manage remote child worker processes. That way, you can spawn worker processes through a network of computers that join a central server process.

A common pitfall of multiprocessing development is the lack of observability in the spawned worker processes. A partial solution is to use the `multiprocessing get_logger()` and `log_to_stderr()` functions, which provide the logger instance used by `multiprocessing`. The issue is that the `logging` module doesn't use locks over the shared logging mechanism, so you could end up with mixed messages.

Finally, multiprocessing can also be executed in an asynchronous way. Python provides high-level mechanisms to execute multi-process solutions, centralized in the `concurrent.futures` module. We are going to explore those capabilities in *Chapter 3*.

In *Chapter 1*, we mentioned that multi-processing is a costly tool that can be outperformed by a more lightweight alternative called multi-threading. A vanilla solution rewritten with multi-processing support will be changed again to test those capabilities in the next section. That way, you will be able to see how Python implements both approaches in a very similar way with different consequences.

Multi-thread solutions

In environments with only one processor, which are the most common ones, instead of spawning costly new processes, you can get better results by using a multi-threaded solution. As mentioned before, the canonical implementation of Python has extensive support and optimizations for this model.

Python's threading module is a set of high-level interfaces over the low-level _thread module. Usually you will rely on the threading module, but if you want to have fine-grained control over operations on threads, the _thread module is the answer. Remember that by using the multi-threading capabilities of Python you are not using all the cores available in modern processors – just one, given the GIL.

Python's threading reading module is wrapped by the multiprocessing.dummy module to offer an API-level compatible Pool subclass (ThreadPool) that implements parallelization work by using threads instead of processes. This way, changing only an import in the Chapter 2/solution4.py file provides the same functionality as previous solutions but uses worker threads instead of worker processes.

In each solution provided, there is a small decorator function (measure_execution_time) that implements a very basic way to measure, in seconds, the execution time for the calculate_path_distance function. It takes the start and end time of the decorated function and prints the difference in seconds. (This method does suffer from some drawbacks, especially in relation to short periods of time. We will discuss better approaches to measuring and comparing performance in *Chapter 5*.)

```python
def measure_execution_time(func):
    def wrapper(*args, **kwargs):
        start_time = time.time()
        result = func(*args, **kwargs)
        end_time = time.time()
        print(f'Function {func} Execution time: {end_time - start_time}
seconds')
        return result
    return wrapper
```

If you review the data provided by our three solutions, you will notice that multi-process/multi-threaded solutions aren't as efficient as simple ones. Why not?

There are several possible reasons. Some might be environmental (processors that perform better under single-core loads rather than multi-core loads or with a particular Python interpreter version/implementation), but the task switching between processes and threads is not negligible, even in operations that seem to be difficult to calculate (recall the great_circle_distance calculation formula). The results of applying multi-processing / multi-threading techniques might be sub-optimal.

Until now, our context problem has been solved using Python's basic toolset for multitasking. Now, what happens when you implement solutions that go beyond the basics and use specific threads? The Python API is flexible, well-documented, and quite comprehensive in this regard, but to realize its full potential you must write thread-safe code, which is discussed in the following section.

Thread safety

Python's threading module provides several utilities to launch and handle a thread's lifecycle, but even so, the most important non-functional requirement that you must address when using it is to ensure the **thread safety** of your solution. Thread-safe code is code that avoids race conditions during execution in multi-threaded environments. There are three commonly accepted levels of thread safety:

1. **Non-thread safe**: There are no guarantees that data structures used in the code can be accessed simultaneously from several threads

2. **Conditionally safe**: Different threads share objects, and access to shared data is protected from race conditions

3. **Thread safe**: There is no shared memory usage, and the data structures used are thread-safe themselves

The following code (Chapter 2/non-safe.py) shows a classic example of non-thread-safe operations. The global variable total is shared among threads that call a function that increments the total by 1. To be sure to illustrate the point, I explicitly added a time.sleep call to the add_to_total function to simulate long-running operations:

```python
import time
import threading


def add_to_total():
    global total
```

```
    for i in range(1000):
        curr = total
        time.sleep(0)
        curr += 1
        total = curr

total = 0
threads = []
for i in range(10):
    t = threading.Thread(target=add_to_total)
    threads.append(t)

for t in threads:
    t.start()

for t in threads:
    t.join()
print(f'{total=}')
```

If you run the code several times, you will notice that the results are inconsistent. Each time the result is different; threads are accessing/writing to the shared variable simultaneously in a non-safe way. To control access to shared objects, the threading module offers several primitive objects:

- **Semaphore**: The oldest access control mechanism, invented by Edsger W. Dijkstra, it is used to control access to limited-capacity resources, such as database connections. The basic idea is that you maintain a number that controls the availability of a resource, and with each acquisition decrease the number. Once released, the number is increased again. This mechanism requires that the control number never goes below zero (0). If it is zero, then the acquisition attempt is rejected.

- **Lock**: Locks are the lowest-level synchronization primitive available. A lock is acquired by a thread explicitly and blocks the execution of any other thread until it is explicitly released. The release operation can be executed not just by the thread that acquired the lock. This requires careful management to avoid releasing a lock that is in place; doing so will produce a RuntimeError. The good news is that the with statement (https://docs. python.org/3/library/threading.html#using-locks-conditions-and-semaphores- in-the-with-statement) acquires the associated lock for the duration of the enclosed block.

- **Condition:** Conditional variables are often used to check several conditions that should be met before acquiring/releasing an implicit lock. For example, in a producer/consumer schema, the producer can acquire the lock using a condition and then once it's finished its operation, notify all other waiting threads that the condition is met to finally release the lock. That way, another of the waiting threads can acquire the lock and keep the execution.

To fix the previous example, the code has been modified (Chapter 2/safe.py) to include a lock that is acquired once the thread is going to operate over the total global variable. In several executions, you will notice that the output is stable:

```python
import time
import threading

def add_to_total():
    global total
    for i in range(1000):
        with lock:
            curr = total
            time.sleep(0)
            curr += 1
            total = curr

total = 0
threads = []
lock = threading.Lock()
for i in range(10):
    t = threading.Thread(target=add_to_total)
    threads.append(t)

for t in threads:
    t.start()

for t in threads:
    t.join()

print(f'{total=}')
```

Thread safety is one of the most complicated challenges in parallel computing. To share data between threads, be sure to use the data structures already provided by Python's API, such as Queue, Deque, and Counter. Doing so will simplify the design, and the cost in performance might be acceptable.

Now that you can inspect your solutions to detect code that might be insecure when executed in a multi-threaded way, let's check the most common use case: **embarrassingly parallel workloads**.

Detecting embarrassingly parallel workloads

Applying a simple function over a loop is a good example of a so-called embarrassingly parallel workload, which means that an easy optimization that can result in improved performance is to use multithreading or multiprocessing techniques to speed up the calculations. More broadly, the basic criterion you should check before trying to implement a parallelization optimization is that the sub-units of work making up your task are completely independent. In the previous example, the distance calculation for cities A and B is completely independent of the B to C case. You can find a simple example of an embarrassingly parallel workload in the repository file Chapter 2/ embarrassingly.py, the code being a simple math operation:

```python
import time
import multiprocessing


def square_number(n):
    time.sleep(0.001)
    return n * n


def serial_square_list(numbers):
    return [square_number(n) for n in numbers]


def parallel_square_list(numbers, num_processes):
    with multiprocessing.Pool(processes=num_processes) as pool:
        results = pool.map(square_number, numbers)
    return results
if name == "main":
    large_list = list(range(10000))
    start_time_serial = time.time()
    serial_results = serial_square_list(large_list)
    end_time_serial = time.time()
```

```
    print(f'Serial squaring finished in: {end_time_serial - start_time_
serial:.4f} seconds')
num_processes = multiprocessing.cpu_count()
    print(f'\nStarting parallel squaring using {num_processes}
processes...')
    start_time_parallel = time.time()
    parallel_results = parallel_square_list(large_list, num_processes)
    end_time_parallel = time.time()
    print(f'Parallel squaring finished in: {end_time_parallel - start_
time_parallel:.4f} seconds')
```

The sample code shows the three characteristics of an embarrassingly parallel workload: independent tasks, minimal communication between tasks, and operational scalability in multiple processors. The comparison between the serial_square_list and parallel_square_list function execution times clearly shows the performance benefit gained from parallelizing this kind of workload.

Not all parallelizable workloads should be parallelized. The costs associated with thread safety and task switching might be higher than the performance gains obtained using multithreading or multiprocessing. A good test suite that includes performance testing and environment isolation can help to evaluate the circumstances. Types of problem which have been identified as being good candidates for parallelization include (among others):

- Monte Carlo simulations: with each experiment being statistically independent, they can be run safely in parallel environments
- Relational database sharding queries: the distribution of queries among distinct nodes in a cluster can accelerate the execution by several times
- Parallel search in constraint programming
- The tree-growth step in random forest algorithms

The Python community has also explored ways to improve the capabilities of the multiprocessing and threading modules offered by the standard API. The Joblib library developed a multiprocessing backend (https://joblib.readthedocs.io/en/latest/parallel.html#serialization-processes) called loky to fix some pitfalls of the default implementation. Other approaches, such as the *Numba* project (https://numba.readthedocs.io/en/stable/user/parallel.html), use techniques such as **just-in-time (JIT) compilation** to apply parallelization automatically.

Summary

In this chapter we have explored the basics of multiprocessing/multithreading applied to a classic embarrassingly parallel problem to discover that the apparently complicated calculations were less of an overhead than the context-switching cost of the parallelization techniques. Then, we discussed the importance of testing thread safety when you work with the `threading` module or similar. Finally, some of the most interesting well-known problems for which parallelization could offer benefits were mentioned. With these tools, you should be able to evaluate whether a workload is a good fit for the application of such kinds of optimization.

The next chapter will go deeper into practice with the implementation of simple solutions that take advantage of Python's cooperative multitasking capabilities: generators and coroutines will be used to improve vanilla solutions for a CPU-intensive problem. Those tools, along with those discussed here, form the basis for understanding the more advanced techniques used to implement asynchronous solutions later.

3

Generators and Coroutines

As Python evolves, it introduces new features and approaches to simplify and enhance the developer experience. In the natural development of the language, two concepts have already been thoughtfully included as a standard part of Python's programming interface: **generators**, as a specialization of **iterators**, and **coroutines**, as a cooperative mechanism applicable in synchronous and asynchronous programming. Generators and coroutines are a natural bridge between synchronous and asynchronous programming. A solid understanding of both will give you a considerable advantage in designing performant solutions in both models.

A common misconception about generators and coroutines is that, by themselves, they will improve the performance of a solution, or that they can be applied to any use case in an uncritical way. To broaden your perspective and extend the previous chapter's early discoveries, we are going to introduce some ways to benchmark your code to (dis)prove biases about implementing solutions using generators and coroutines.

Specifically, in this chapter, we're going to cover the following main topics:

- Understanding generators and coroutines
- Introducing Python **performance benchmarking**
- Using coroutines in asynchronous programming

Technical requirements

In this chapter we will be using some external packages to illustrate the concepts discussed. First, we will use a **server-sent event (SSE)** client library (`sseclient`) to consume a data stream. Then, to extend the default Python profiling capabilities, we will add the `pyinstrument` module.

It is not a requirement to understand or test the code available in the Chapter03 folder of the GitHub repo (https://github.com/PacktPublishing/Asynchronous-Programming-in-Python), but it will let you compare the extended profiling features. Finally, a synthetic data provider library will help with building some common attributes for custom data. Remember to generate a virtual environment exclusively for the chapter. That way, the additional packages will not interfere with other requirements:

```
$ python3 -m venv .env
$ source .env/bin/activate
$ pip install -r requirements.txt
```

Understanding generators and coroutines

Iteration is one of the basic operations in imperative programming. Besides iterating over the standard data structures provided by the Python programming interface, you can develop your own iterator classes. These must implement the iterator contract, which involves implementing the __iter__ and __next__ methods.

The following code, available at Chapter 3/iterators.py, implements an iterator over a fictional soccer team's members. Data is generated on-the-fly to look like real data; this *synthetic data* could be used for integration tests, in which you want data that is close to real data in terms of format and statistical properties but which is otherwise unrelated to real data (usually for compliance and/or security reasons).

```python
from faker import Faker
class SoccerTeam():
    def __init__(self):
        fake = Faker()
        self.players = [fake.name() for _ in range(11)]
        self.current = 0

    def __iter__(self):
        return self

    def __next__(self):
        if self.current >= len(self.players):
            raise StopIteration
        else:
            player = self.players[self.current]
```

```
            self.current += 1
            return self.current, player


st = SoccerTeam()
st_iterator = iter(st)
num, curr_player = next(st_iterator)
print(f'Goalkeeper {num}: {curr_player}')
for n, cp in st:
    print(f'Player {n}: {cp}')
```

The code is fairly simple. The SoccerTeam class keeps a list of the names of the 11 players and implements the two methods required to comply with the *iterator* contract. Check the st_iterator = iter(st) line, in which an iterator instance is instantiated through Python's iter(iterable_object) function. That method represents syntactic sugar to call the __iter__ method. Then, for each call to the next() function, the __next__ method will be called and the indexer of the internal list in the SoccerTeam instance will be updated. Notice that iteration over fixed-size data structures raises a StopIteration exception once you try to go over the limits of the iterator. Now that the contract to implement a custom iterator is clear, let's extend the idea down to generators.

Generators are a specialization of iterators. The idea is that you don't have to iterate over a fixed data structure. In the previous example, we used the SoccerTeam.players list, but instead you can generate/use only the most recent element every time you require it. The following code (available at Chapter 3/generators.py) shows a simple implementation of a SoccerTeam generator:

```
from faker import Faker
def soccer_team():
    fake = Faker()
    for current in range(11):
        yield current, fake.name()
        current += 1


st = soccer_team()
num, curr_player = next(st)
print(f'Goalkeeper {num}: {curr_player}')
for n, cp in st:
    print(f'Player {n}: {cp}')
```

This code is even simpler than the previous iterator version. It doesn't include the __iter__ and __next__ methods but instead introduces the yield expression, which acts like a **partial return** for the function.

Partial return means that the function gives back control to the caller but keeps the state of execution of the function up to that point – in our example, the value of the current local variable inside of the loop. That way, when you call the function to resume execution through the next() statement or through the for ... in loop, Python will not restart but rather will restore the state and execute from that point.

Python also has generator comprehension syntax, which lets you define one-liner generators. For example, you can replace the previous generator function with a generator expression such as the following:

```
st = ((_,fake.name()) for _ in range(11))
```

Notice that the generator expression uses parentheses instead of the square brackets or braces used in list and dictionary comprehensions.

If we go one step further, we can ask what happens if we need to not only extract data from the generator function but also give it arguments to resume its execution. These arguments are not part of the function but are necessary to achieve its purpose. That's the original idea behind coroutines – generator functions that can have not only partial results but also partial arguments. The following example (available at Chapter 3/coroutine.py) illustrates the concept by using a generator as part of a simulation, instead of reading the data from an Internet of the Things (IoT) sensor or an external service, which is an approach that might be useful for testing or modeling purposes:

```python
import numpy as np
def sim_temp(mean:float=15, stdv:float=5):
    rng = np.random.default_rng()
    temps = [rng.normal(mean, stdv) for _ in range(365)]
    yield min(temps), max(temps)
    threshold = (yield)
    print(f'Threshold: {threshold}')
    days_over_threshold = len([d for d in temps if d > threshold])
    print(f'There were: {days_over_threshold} days over {threshold}
degrees')
    yield days_over_threshold


m = 22
std = 8
s = sim_temp(m, std)
```

```
print(f'Simulating the temp around {m} with standard deviation of {std}')
min, max = s.__next__()
print(f'The temp moves between {min} and {max} centigrades')
s.__next__()
s.send((max-min)/2)
```

In this example, the sim_temp coroutine function uses NumPy's normal distribution generator to simulate temperatures around a mean and standard deviation given as arguments to the function. Then it partially returns the minimum and maximum values of the generated list and waits for a threshold value. Once it gets it, it calculates how many values are greater than that threshold. The co-operation of the main thread and the coroutine might be a little confusing, but you can understand it by following the execution sequence:

1. The **main thread** declares the median, standard deviation, and **coroutine**. The code of the **coroutine** is not executed yet.

2. The **main thread** prints the first message.

3. The **main thread** passes the control to the **coroutine** using the __next__() method.

4. The **coroutine** executes the code until the first yield statement.

5. The **coroutine** returns control to the **main thread**.

6. The **main thread** assigns the values returned by the **coroutine** to the min and max variables.

7. The **main thread** prints the second message.

8. The **main thread** passes the control again to the **coroutine** with the second __next__() function call.

9. The **coroutine** expects a value for the threshold variable, so it returns control to the **main thread** and waits until a send() function is called.

10. The **main thread** provides the value to the **coroutine** and again gives control to it.

11. The **coroutine** uses list comprehension to calculate the days over the threshold, prints the message, and finally returns the control to the **main thread**.

Notice that sim_temp combines both generator and coroutine capabilities – min and max values are calculated on the fly based on the simulated temperatures (you can think of an alternative version in which the temperatures are read from an external source or stream). The generator function keeps its state after the first yield expression is reached, and once the caller thread has used the send() function to provide the required partial arguments it continues its execution.

Coroutines also can gracefully handle the overflow of __next__() calls, using the return clause and StopIteration/GeneratorExit exceptions. The following code (available at Chapter 3/ coroutineExceptions.py) shows this behavior management:

```python
import numpy as np


def sim_temp(mean:float=15, stdv:float=5):
    try:
        rng = np.random.default_rng()
        temps = [rng.normal(mean, stdv) for _ in range(365)]
        yield min(temps), max(temps)
        threshold = (yield)
        print(f'Threshold: {threshold}')
        days_over_threshold = len([d for d in temps if d > threshold])
        print(f'There were:{days_over_threshold} days over {threshold}
degrees')
        yield days_over_threshold
    except GeneratorExit:
        print('This is already closed')
        return 0
try:
    m = 22
    std = 8
    s = sim_temp(m, std)
    print(f'Simulating the temp around {m} with standard deviation of
{std}')
    min, max = s.__next__()
    s.close()
    print(f'The temp moves between {min} and {max} centigrades')
    s.__next__()
    s.send((max-min)/2)
except StopIteration:
    print('Nothing else in the coroutine')
```

The counter coroutine is requested to stop early by the main thread (notice the s.close() line) but is later called again using the __next__() statement, which will raise a StopIteration function that is handled by the main thread.

The cooperation shown in previous coroutine examples is synchronous. We haven't created any new threads or processes to execute the coroutines/generators, but before going into how to use coroutines in an asynchronous way, let's get a better understanding of how to measure the gains of applying new techniques to existing solutions. More specifically, we'll look at how to use Python tools to measure the time and resources that generators, threads, or coroutines use during their execution.

Introducing Python performance benchmarking

Every software solution has associated costs. Solutions consume computational resources and also have an associated level of complexity that has implications for runtime performance. The parameters relevant to measuring Python code execution include time taken, CPU cycles used, memory allocation, network bandwidth, and persistent storage usage. We are going to focus on time and memory. Time can be measured in many ways; usually you can obtain measures of CPU time and *wall time*. CPU time measures the duration of actual computation, excluding the overheads of waiting and task switching (which, as we have already shown, has important consequences). Wall time, meanwhile, includes all the subtasks required to execute a piece of code.

The following code uses the perf_counter() function from the time module to compare two implementations of an approximation function for calculating the value of pi (3.14159265...):

```python
import time

def pi_approximation(terms):
    denominator = 1.0
    sign = 1.0
    result = 0.0
    for _ in range(terms):
        result += sign * (4.0 / denominator)
        sign *= -1
        denominator += 2

    return result

def pi_approximation_generator(terms):
    denominator = 1.0
    sign = 1.0
    result = 0.0
```

```python
    for _ in range(terms):
        result += sign * (4.0 / denominator)
        sign *= -1
        denominator += 2
        yield result


if __name__ == '__main__':
    num_iters = 1000000
    for i in range(3):
        start = time.process_time_ns()
        pi_approx = pi_approximation(num_iters)
        end = time.process_time_ns()
        print(f'PI: {pi_approx} took {(end - start)/1000000000} seconds')
        start = time.process_time_ns()
        for approx in pi_approximation_generator(num_iters):
            pi_approx = approx
        end = time.process_time_ns()
        print(f'PIusing generator: {pi_approx} {(end - start)/1000000000}
seconds')
```

The perf_counter() uses a *'clock with the highest available resolution to measure a short duration'* (https://docs.python.org/3/library/time.html#time.perf_counter) that measures the wall time of the execution. You will notice that the generator version takes slightly more time than the traditional one. This is because it has to handle the overhead of yielding and resuming execution on each iteration. This process of pausing and resuming adds a small, but cumulatively not insignificant, performance cost. If you want to check the difference with respect to the CPU time, you can compare the results of the process_time_ns() function. This way of measuring execution time is highly coupled to the code, which is less than ideal, so we are going to use an alternative that's more suitable for measuring short pieces of code.

Using a less simple code execution timer

Python's timeit module provides a programmatic interface like the time module but also a command-line interface suitable for checking small pieces of code. It provides the means to control certain aspects of the code, such as the number of iterations over which the observed code must be run or the number of times the measurement must be repeated. The following code shows how to run the previous functions from the command line, measuring their execution:

```
$ python3 -m timeit -n 100 -s "import PiTime; PiTime.pi_
approximation(1000000)"
100 loops, best of 5: 8.22 nsec per loop
$ python3 -m timeit -n 100 -s "import PiTime; PiTime.pi_approximation_
generator(1000000)"
100 loops, best of 5: 8.12 nsec per loop
```

The timeit module decouples simple wall time measurement from the code but still makes it slightly effortful to get more than direct time tracking. For scenarios in which the code to be measured is not trivial you need more advanced tools, especially if you are going to compare synchronous and asynchronous code versions.

Statistically profiling your code

Well-known in physics, the *observer effect* also occurs in computer science. Observing a system alters its behavior to a greater or lesser extent, and this happens when you profile a program. Some resources are assigned to the profiler itself, modifying the behavior of the code that is expected to be profiled. To minimize the effect of profiling on actual code execution you can use a profiler that doesn't record *all* the states of the observed code but instead uses statistical sampling methods to obtain profiling data over time.

In the Python ecosystem you find both kinds of profiler. The most common one, **cProfile**, has noticeable impacts on some programs. There are community alternatives, such as **py-spy**, which uses sampling to reduce the overhead and also supports multithreading profiling. The following code (available as Chapter 3/divisors.py) shows a multithread implementation that finds the divisors of a large number:

```python
import threading
import logging

def divisors_without_generator(number):
    divisors = []
    for divisor in range(1, number + 1):
        if number % divisor == 0:
            divisors.append(divisor)
    logging.info(f'Divisors of {number}: {divisors}')

def divisors_with_generator(number):
    for divisor in range(1, number + 1):
```

```
        if number % divisor == 0:
            yield divisor

def divisors_consumer(number):
    for d in divisors_with_generator(number):
        logging.info(f'{d} is divisor of {number}')

def find_divisors_threaded(number):
    thread1 = threading.Thread(target=divisors_consumer, args=(number,))
    thread2 = threading.Thread(target=divisors_consumer, args=(number*5,))
    thread3 = threading.Thread(target=divisors_without_generator,
args=(number,))
    thread4 = threading.Thread(target=divisors_without_generator,
args=(number*5,))

    thread1.start()
    thread2.start()
    thread3.start()
    thread4.start()

    thread1.join()
    thread2.join()
    thread3.join()
    thread4.join()

if __name__ == '__main__':
    logging.basicConfig(level=logging.INFO, format='%(threadName)s:
%(message)s')
    find_divisors_threaded(10000000)
```

To check execution times per thread you can run the code using the **py-spy** record mode. This will generate an interactive SVG file that shows the actual execution time per thread call as a flame chart:

```
$ py-spy record -o profile.svg -- python3 divisors.py
```

The result is shown in the following figure:

py-spy record -o profile.svg -- python3 divisors.py

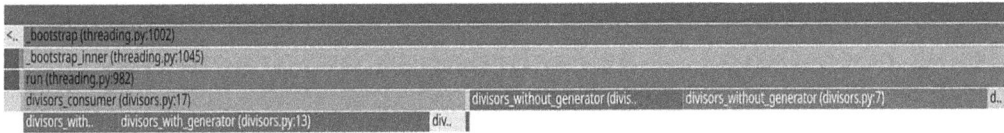

Figure 3.1: Flame graph of execution times for a multithreaded program

Notice that the generator and non-generator functions are actually divided to run concurrently, given that they are executed in different threads. This type of visualization facilitates analysis of the impact of multithreading solutions and comparisons against different implementations. But there are also other visualization modes that can facilitate analysis of the execution time – for example, you can view the data as a table:

```
Collecting samples from 'python divisors.py' (python v3.11.10)
Total Samples 100
GIL: 96.67%, Active: 104.44%, Threads: 3
```

%Own	%Total	OwnTime	TotalTime	Function (filename)
53.33%	53.33%	0.520s	0.520s	divisors_without_generator (divisors.py
46.67%	46.67%	0.490s	0.490s	divisors_with_generator (divisors.py)
4.44%	4.44%	0.040s	0.040s	_wait_for_tstate_lock (threading.py)
0.00%	100.00%	0.000s	1.01s	_bootstrap_inner (threading.py)
0.00%	100.00%	0.000s	1.01s	run (threading.py)
0.00%	4.44%	0.000s	0.040s	join (threading.py)
0.00%	4.44%	0.000s	0.040s	<module> (divisors.py)
0.00%	46.67%	0.000s	0.490s	divisors_consumer (divisors.py)
0.00%	100.00%	0.000s	1.01s	_bootstrap (threading.py)
0.00%	4.44%	0.000s	0.040s	find_divisors_threaded (divisors.py)

Figure 3.2: Table of execution times for a multithreaded program

It is also interesting to measure memory, given the amount of data that it is now customary to work with. (Long gone are the days when '*640K ought to be enough for anybody*' – https://www.computerworld.com/article/1563853/the-640k-quote-won-t-go-away-but-did-gates-really-say-it.html). Also because in Function-as-a-Service environments you get billed by the amount of RAM that you use. There are many community tools that support memory profiling, such as **memray** (https://github.com/bloomberg/memray). The rule of thumb is that generators should be more memory-efficient than fixed-length data structures, since they keep only the current value being processed.

Now that we have a non-intrusive tool that can measure time in a consistent way and which is suitable for synchronous and asynchronous implementations, in the next section we'll use it to measure asynchronous coroutines.

Using coroutines in asynchronous programming

Coroutines have evolved to be the unit of concurrency in asynchronous programming in Python. Because they are executed in a single thread they are not constrained by the global interpreter lock (GIL), and task switching is more lightweight than the same operation executed on threads or processes. Coroutines are suitable for many modern use cases that involve non-blocking I/O operations over data streams or network connections.

Support for asynchronous coroutines has also evolved. In early versions of Python (up to CPython 3.4), the recommended way to develop asynchronous capabilities for coroutines was to use the @asyncio.coroutine decorator over coroutine functions. This changed with the inclusion of the asyncio module in CPython 3.4 and the addition of the async/await expressions in CPython 3.5.

> **Important note**
>
> Since the asyncio.coroutine decorator has been deprecated in CPython 3.8 and removed in 3.11, we are going to directly use the asyncio capabilities and recommend migrating any code that still keeps the previous syntax.

The **asyncio** module will be covered in detail in *Chapter 4*. Meanwhile, assume that it provides a context and a scheduler for coroutine functions, i.e. asyncio encapsulates coroutine functions as tasks. Code execution of those tasks can be awaited, and when they have finished the result is returned or an exception is raised. This context manager for coroutines is called the **event loop** and you won't usually deal directly with it unless you want to extend it or customize its behavior to build a library/framework around it. The following code (available as Chapter 3/sseClient.py) shows the main() coroutine's characteristics in asynchronous programming:

```
import json
import asyncio
from sseclient import SSEClient

messages = SSEClient('https://stream.wikimedia.org/v2/stream/
recentchange')
batch_size = 3
```

```
vals = []

async def sse_client_get_values():
    batch = []
    for event in messages:
        if event.event == 'message':
            try:
                change = json.loads(event.data)
            except ValueError:
                pass
            else:
                if change['meta']['domain'] == 'canary' or change['bot']
== True:
                    continue
                if len(batch) < batch_size:
                    batch.append(change['user'])
                else:
                    return batch

async def fetcher():
    while True:
        io_vals = await sse_client_get_values()
        vals.extend(io_vals)
        await asyncio.sleep(1)

async def monitor():
    while True:
        print (vals)
        await asyncio.sleep(1)

async def main():
    t1 = asyncio.create_task(fetcher())
    t2 = asyncio.create_task(monitor())
    await asyncio.gather(t1, t2)

asyncio.run(main())
```

The example uses a main() coroutine to simultaneously run a producer and a consumer. The fetcher() coroutine acts as a data producer from an external data stream and the monitor() coroutine accesses the results of the production.

The actual data source in this case is a server-sent event (SSE) data stream provided by the Wikimedia Foundation that pushes a JSON object with metadata about recent changes to consumers. Our sse_client_get_values() coroutine filters the messages that are from non-canary servers and produced by humans to return batches of three.

Our fetcher() coroutine awaits the end of sse_client_get_values() (returning a new batch) and adds its values to a global list, vals, before putting itself in a wait state using the non-blocking asyncio.sleep() function. The event loop takes this time to execute the other coroutine, monitor(), which accesses the globally shared resource vals.

Let's analyze in some detail the coroutine characteristics of this code:

- Coroutines must be explicitly defined using the async def clause.
- Coroutines are actually executed once you await them.
- You can run coroutines simultaneously awaiting the asyncio.gather() method, which awaits each element individually and returns a list with each coroutine result. In this case, given that our fetcher() and monitor() coroutines run forever, we don't process the results.

Notice that this asynchronous version of coroutines (called native coroutines) differs from simple coroutines in several respects:

- They run inside the asyncio event loop (check the asyncio.run(main()) call in the previous example)
- They don't use the yield statement but instead the traditional return statement
- They don't use the yield statement to gather partial arguments as simple coroutines but instead await other coroutines

There are several reasons to use coroutines, but a common assumption about them is that they will instantly improve performance. We are going to examine this assumption in the next section.

Are coroutines faster than threads/processes?

Throwing async into any function and running through the asyncio event loop won't give you instant performance gains. In some cases, it might make your solution slower or less predictable.

You could expect that your code would be less prone to race conditions when you access shared resources (remember that the event loop executes only one coroutine at a time, even if multiple coroutines start to run simultaneously), but from the performance point of view, and, more specifically, the wall time measurement, you have to consider several factors that can affect coroutines:

- The type of load (CPU-bound or I/O-bound)
- The number of simultaneous tasks you will launch (threads usually support tens of thousands per core; coroutines can go over hundreds of thousands)
- The type of I/O resources you will access in your tasks – remember that coroutines are specialized in non-blocking I/O operations such as data streams, so using coroutines to access shared blocking I/O resources might degrade the overall performance
- The execution environment (vCPUs from cloud providers? FaaS environments? Local processors?)

Jason Brownlee set an interesting benchmark (available at `https://superfastpython.com/asyncio-coroutines-faster-than-threads/`) when he considered several of these aspects in a blog post. His results are counterintuitive in some cases, but you should get your own results, since the conditions in which you execute your code might be different enough to get distinct values. For example, recent versions of CPython have included many performance enhancements (the version 3.11 release notes claim gains of between 10% and 60% over version 3.10 in some cases). The introduction of just-in-time compilation since version 3.13 can also lead to better performance.

Summary

Simple generators/coroutines are constructs that can be heavily used in synchronous programming to improve use cases in which you have to deal with large data structures. The principal benefit of understanding those concepts is that you gain access to cooperative execution without too much hassle. Also, it prepares the ground for extending the coroutines' capabilities into Python's standard asynchronous programming interface. In this chapter, we have introduced `asyncio` module basics that let coroutines be executed asynchronously and give you some tooling to measure performance in an unobtrusive way.

The next chapter will go deeper into the `asyncio` module, exploring not only coroutines but also other types of awaitable objects that open the door to model solutions beyond the scope of coroutines. In addition we will revisit the concept of coroutines by implementing them in other execution contexts distinct from the standard `asyncio` context.

Get This Book's PDF Version and Exclusive Extras

4

Implementing Coroutines with Asyncio and Trio

Asynchronous coroutines are Python's current state-of-the-art cooperative multitasking feature. In this chapter we are going to formalize our understanding of **asyncio**, starting with the concepts required to work with the module, and then use those concepts in a working example. Later, we'll discuss some advanced techniques such as asynchronous iterators, comprehensions, and unit testing. Next, two alternatives to the standard library will be presented, since coroutines can be implemented in different ways. This chapter provides the understanding necessary to design and develop the more complex solutions that will be presented in *Chapters 7 to 10*, and covers the following main topics:

- Using asyncio to implement coroutines
- Exploring **Trio** – an alternative for asynchronous coroutines

Technical requirements

In this chapter we use a number of external packages besides the standard Python library to explore Trio, an alternative to asyncio. In addition, we will use server-sent event (SSE) blocking and non-blocking client libraries to consume a data stream, and then other support libraries for input/output operations will be used. The source code is available in the Chapter04 folder of the GitHub repo (https://github.com/PacktPublishing/Asynchronous-Programming-in-Python). Remember to generate a virtual environment exclusively for the chapter, so that the additional packages do not interfere with other requirements:

```
$ python3 -m venv .env
$ pip install -r requirements.txt
```

Using asyncio to implement coroutines

Asyncio is the default implementation in Python of an **event loop** for asynchronous input/output operations. An event loop is a pattern that solves the problem of concurrent access to shared resources. In 1965, the famous computer scientist Edsger W. Dijkstra formulated a problem called 'The dining philosophers', which goes something like this:

> *Five philosophers dine together at the same table. Each philosopher has their own plate at the table. There is a fork between each pair of adjacent plates. The dish served is a kind of spaghetti which has to be eaten with two forks. Each philosopher can only alternately think and eat. Moreover, a philosopher can only eat their spaghetti when they have both a left and right fork. Thus, two forks will only be available when their two nearest neighbors are thinking, not eating. After an individual philosopher finishes eating, they will put down both forks.*
>
> *(Wikipedia:* https://en.wikipedia.org/wiki/Dining_philosophers_problem*)*

The challenge is to design an algorithm that allows each philosopher to alternately eat/think forever without starving any of the philosophers. Shared resources (forks) must be managed in such a way that they serve all the (possibly increasing number of) clients.

The event loop is effectively a loop that takes advantage of coroutines' characteristics in order to do the following:

- Schedule code execution
- Execute callbacks
- Perform network input/output
- Run subprocesses

The event loop pattern is also implemented in other languages, such as JavaScript, where it is the basis for the high-performance Node.js runtime. *Figure 4.1* shows an approximation of how several coroutines are managed by an event loop:

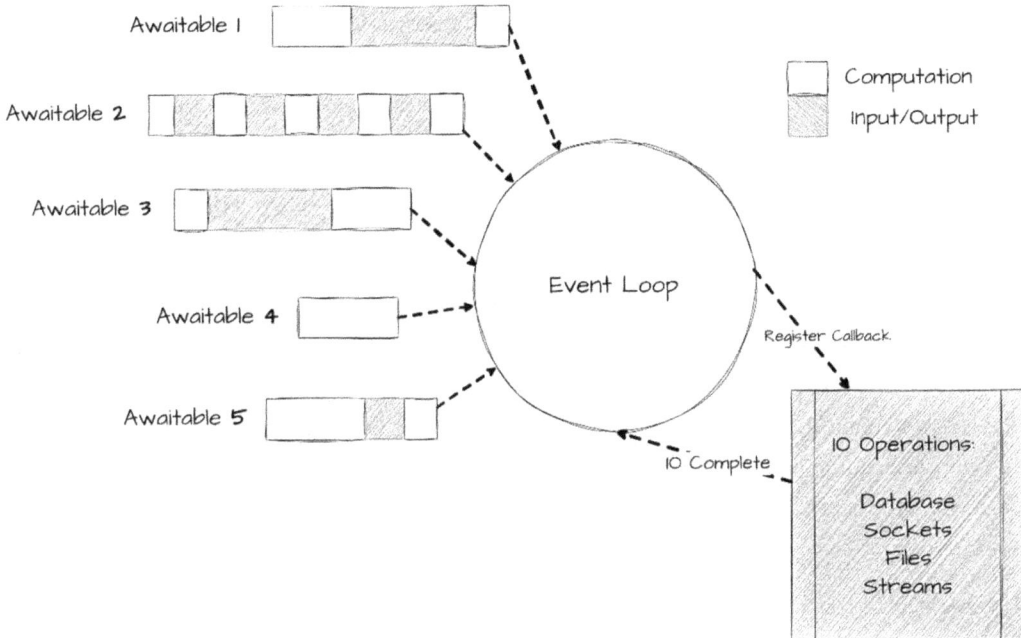

Figure 4.1: Event loop execution

Execution time for tasks can, to a first approximation, be decomposed into computation time and input/output (I/O) wait time. The event loop schedules the task to be run and suspends its execution once there is an I/O operation in the code; then when the task's I/O operation is done the scheduler resumes its execution to complete the task. This pattern performs best when I/O operations are non-blocking. In this way, coroutines react to the flux of data from streams, sockets, or file operations.

Strictly speaking, asyncio is a module that allows Python code to handle tasks through an event loop implementation. It also provides a way to create modules to execute asynchronous I/O operations, which are usually provided by third-party packages. *Chapters 7 to 10* explore specific scenarios in which those I/O packages are heavily used.

To be able to properly use the event loop pattern, you have to ensure that the tasks that are handled don't block the thread. Otherwise, all other tasks will have to wait until the blocking operation releases the main thread. You may ask yourself: What if I have a library/code/algorithm that is not async native? Well, as we will explore in the *Putting asyncio into action* section, you have to be aware of this and use threads.

We variously invoke the terms **coroutines, tasks,** and **awaitables** when we talk about operations that are handled by the event loop, but the terms are not exactly equivalent. In asyncio, each operation handled is a task. Those tasks can be 'awaited' to be completed, so they are a kind of object known as awaitables. The next section explains the ways in which you can create awaitables on your own. Spoiler alert: high-level coroutines are awaitables.

Understanding awaitables

Before starting to code using asyncio, we're going to dig a little bit into the concept of an awaitable object, which is the contract asyncio expects to be implemented by the tasks it has to handle. Formally speaking, there are no interfaces in Python 3 (as a means to establish a code contract that classes implementing the interface have to adhere to), but with **Abstract Base Classes (ABCs)** you can get a similar behavior. In this case, Awaitable is an ABC defined in the collections.abc package (https://docs.python.org/3/library/collections.abc.html#collections.abc.Awaitable).

The Awaitable contract defines that classes must implement an __await()__ method which should return an iterator object that is consumed by the event loop, yielding values until the iterator is exhausted. Each yielded value can be another awaitable object, allowing for the chaining of await expressions. There are three standard implementations of the ABC Awaitable: Coroutine, Future, and Task. *Figure 4.2* shows you a simple class diagram that illustrates this fact:

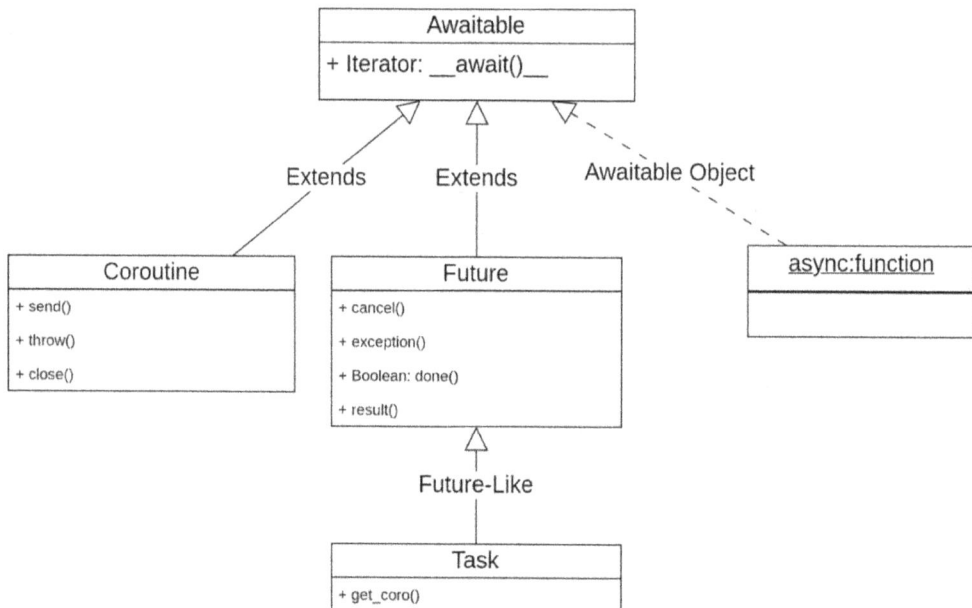

Figure 4.2: Awaitable class hierarchy approximation

The Coroutine ABC defines helper methods to implement communication along with the coroutine. They can only be awaited once. If you try to await them once they have finished their execution, an exception will be thrown. When awaited, they run their code in a task, finally returning a value or throwing an exception.

Future represents non-thread-safe operations that have a result eventually or which can throw an exception. (Thread safety is an important detail that you must consider – check out *Chapter 2* for an introduction to the topic.) They can be awaited multiple times. Future includes a method called done() that returns true if the Future is done or has been canceled, or if its result has been set explicitly. Asyncio's Future should not be confused with concurrent.futures.Future (a class that encapsulates the asynchronous execution of a callable), which is not awaitable.

The Task class is a specialization of Future that encapsulates coroutines to be executed by an event loop, which is also the preferred way to instantiate a Task using the high-level asyncio. create_task() API function or the low-level loop.create_task(). Being a subclass of Future, Task is not thread-safe, and you should be careful with shared resource management (especially I/O operations) when using it.

Note that you can also implement the Awaitable ABC, but to get an awaitable object you can also define a function with the async keyword to transform it into a coroutine. That flexibility simplifies the usage of asyncio in object-oriented programming and in REPL/functional programming.

In the next section, we will implement a complete example to demonstrate the principal features of the asyncio package, including non-blocking I/O and the advanced topic of mixing blocking operations in asynchronous contexts.

Putting asyncio into action

Let's extend the *Chapter 3* example in which we consumed a data stream and monitored that operation using coroutines. We concurrently executed the fetcher and the monitor, just to illustrate the basic idea behind asyncio. Now we want to extend the example to serialize the data that is fetched from the stream into local JSON files. *Figure 4.3* illustrates the solution:

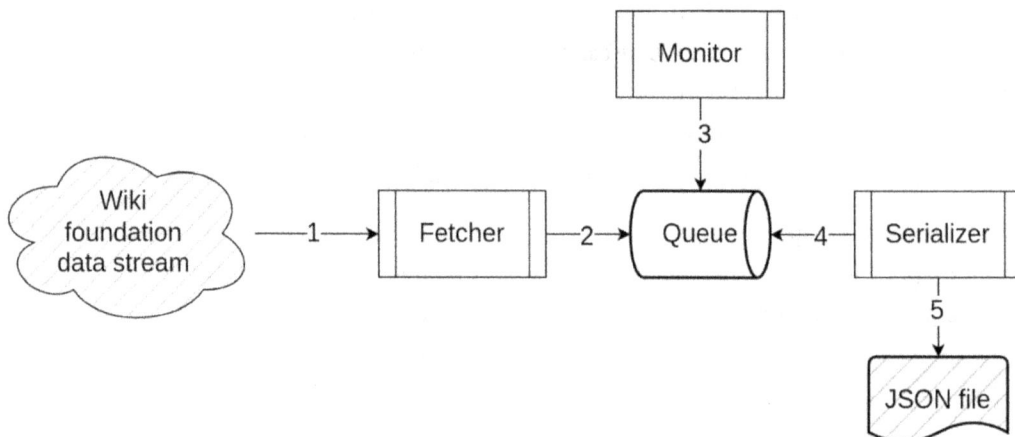

Figure 4.3: Awaitable class hierarchy approximation

The expected flow of the program is as follows:

1. The fetcher coroutine listens to the data stream.
2. The fetcher coroutine puts a batch of messages into a queue to be serialized.
3. The monitor coroutine logs the current size of the queue in the console.
4. A new serializer coroutine consumes the messages in the queue.
5. The serializer coroutine writes the content of each message into a text file in JSON format.

The following code shows a possible implementation of the above design:

```
import json
import queue
import asyncio
from sseclient import SSEClient

messages = SSEClient('https://stream.wikimedia.org/v2/stream/
recentchange')
batch_size = 3
max_vals = 10
```

```
vals = queue.Queue(maxsize=max_vals)

async def sse_client_get_values():
    batch = []
    for event in messages:
        if event.event == 'message':
            try:
                change = json.loads(event.data)
            except ValueError:
                pass
            else:
                if change['meta']['domain'] == 'canary' or change['bot']
== True:
                    continue
                if len(batch) < batch_size:
                    batch.append(change)
                else:
                    return batch

async def fetcher():
    while True:
        io_vals = await sse_client_get_values()
        try:
            for item in io_vals:
                vals.put(item, block=False)
        except queue.Full:
            print("Queue is full")
            return True
        await asyncio.sleep(1)

async def monitor():
    while True:
        curr_len = vals.qsize()
        if curr_len >= max_vals:
            return True
        else:
            print("Queue size:",curr_len)
```

```python
        await asyncio.sleep(1)

async def serializer():
    while True:
        try:
            item = vals.get_nowait()
            print("item read, Wiki edited by:", item["user"])
            f = open(f'./tmp/${item["id"]}.json', "a")
            json.dump(item, f)
            f.close()
        except queue.Empty:
            print("Queue is empty")
            return True
        await asyncio.sleep(1)

async def main():
    t1 = asyncio.create_task(fetcher())
    t2 = asyncio.create_task(monitor())
    t3 = asyncio.create_task(serializer())
    await asyncio.gather(t1, t2, t3)

asyncio.run(main())
```

You will notice that in this version we have put a limit on the size of the queue, via the max_vals variable, and that the three coroutines have exit conditions based on the size of the shared resource (the queue size). The code is basically the same as the solution presented in *Chapter 3*. We have created three tasks using the high-level asyncio API and awaited them to be run concurrently by the event loop.

The fetcher coroutine delegates the actual SSE consumption into another coroutine, but instead of putting the result into a list, it enqueues the entire message into the global queue. The new serializer coroutine takes one message at a time from the global queue and serializes it into a file.

Notice that the exceptions raised by the queue are being caught in the coroutines. When the queue is full or empty the code exits, printing a message to the console. If you execute the code, you will get something like this:

```
Queue size: 3
item read, Wiki edited by: Chabe01
```

```
Queue size: 5
item read, Wiki edited by: 2601:642:4A00:2E60:2CF6:FFDB:DF5A:16D9
Queue size: 7
item read, Wiki edited by: Ceslause
Queue size: 9
item read, Wiki edited by: JuanCamacho
Queue is full
item read, Wiki edited by: NoonIcarus
item read, Wiki edited by: 199.250.9.218
item read, Wiki edited by: MB-one
item read, Wiki edited by: Malkawi99
item read, Wiki edited by: MB-one
item read, Wiki edited by: Tom.Reding
item read, Wiki edited by: NoonIcarus
item read, Wiki edited by: Vmzp85
item read, Wiki edited by: Aquillion
item read, Wiki edited by: WhatamIdoing
Queue is empty
```

While the three coroutines run asynchronously, this solution has a common issue in the first and last step: it uses blocking input (reading the data from the stream) and output (serializing messages to a file) operations. This implies that the main thread will wait until the entire batch of messages is read from the stream (which can take an unknown amount of time) and that it will also block the thread when writing a message to a file.

This flaw in the implementation is a common one. In many designs, concurrent operations end up using standard packages that block the entire execution thread, actually eliminating the gains of an asynchronous design. How can you fix this? Usually, the best solution is to take advantage of libraries designed to operate in an asynchronous context. In this case, we are going to fix the issues by using a non-blocking client to consume SSEs and a non-blocking file writer:

```
import json
import queue
import asyncio
import aiofiles
from aiosseclient import aiosseclient

max_vals = 10
```

```python
vals = queue.Queue(maxsize=max_vals)
fetch_done = False


async def fetcher():
    while True:
        try:
            async for item in aiosseclient('https://stream.wikimedia.org/
v2/stream/recentchange'):
                vals.put(json.loads(item.data), block=False)
                await asyncio.sleep(1)
        except queue.Full:
            print("Queue is full")
            return True


async def monitor():
    while True:
        curr_len = vals.qsize()
        if curr_len >= max_vals:
            fetch_done = True
            return True
        else:
            print("Queue size:",curr_len)
        await asyncio.sleep(1)


async def serializer():
    while True:
        try:
            item = vals.get_nowait()
            print("item read, Wiki edited by:", item["user"])
            async with aiofiles.open(f'./tmp/${item["id"]}.json',
mode='w') as f:
                await f.write(json.dumps(item))
        except queue.Empty:
            print("Queue is empty")
            if fetch_done == True:
                return True
        await asyncio.sleep(1)
```

```
async def main():
    t1 = asyncio.create_task(fetcher())
    t2 = asyncio.create_task(monitor())
    t3 = asyncio.create_task(serializer())
    await asyncio.gather(t1, t2, t3)

asyncio.run(main())
```

In this case the `aiosseclient` and `aiofiles` libraries bring asynchronous input/output capabilities, consuming the data stream and queueing the message each time it is produced and writing the JSON dump into the file. This implementation also has an interesting subsequent problem; if you execute the code, you will see something like:

```
Queue size: 0
Queue is empty
Queue size: 0
Queue is empty
Queue size: 1
item read, Wiki edited by: KrBot
Queue size: 1
item read, Wiki edited by: Eternalwisee
Queue size: 1
item read, Wiki edited by: AnRo0002
Queue size: 1
```

This makes it evident that the exit condition will never be met for the fetcher/monitor coroutines. Once a message arrives, it is queued and also consumed by the serializer, and eventually you will have an empty queue, and thus the serializer will stop. There are many ways to fix this, including long polling or blocking queues, but keep your solution consistent with the sync/async paradigm that you are implementing. One of the more error-prone choices you can make is to mix sync and async code in a solution.

What if you are in a corner and have to mix blocking code in an asynchronous solution? Asyncio's high-level `asyncio.to_thread()` API function creates an instance of type `ThreadPoolExecutor` to execute the I/O blocking code in a separate thread and returns a coroutine that can be awaited. While this approach is valid for I/O blocking operations, you might also need to use the low-level event loop `loop.run_in_executor` API function.

Once you have designed your solution to use asyncio's capabilities, you can explore further optimizations provided by third-party libraries, such as the **uvloop** project. A drop-in replacement for the asyncio event loop, it provides performance gains of orders of magnitude (check the benchmarks at `http://magic.io/blog/uvloop-blazing-fast-python-networking/`), not only for the standard asyncio features but also for third-party extensions such as **aiohttp**.

Now that we have some understanding of how to use asyncio, let's explore a different approach to running asynchronous code: by using the Trio package, which implements the concept of **structured concurrency**.

Exploring Trio

Some time ago, between Python versions 3.6 and 3.11, an interesting alternative implementation of the event loop emerged from the community, led by Nathaniel J. Smith, to handle particular cases in which asyncio shows some rough edges.

Trio (`https://trio.readthedocs.io/en/stable/index.html`) gained attention by, among other things, implementing a 'nursery' mechanism. A detailed explanation of the problem that nurseries solve is available at `https://vorpus.org/blog/notes-on-structured-concurrency-or-go-statement-considered-harmful/#nurseries-a-structured-replacement-for-go-statements`. There it is stated that a parent thread should not let child tasks run without first creating a safe execution environment – the so-called **nursery**. Before going forward, let's adapt our asyncio source code for Trio:

```
import trio
import json
import queue
import httpx
from httpx_sse import connect_sse

max_vals = 10
vals = queue.Queue(maxsize=max_vals)
fetch_done = False

async def fetcher():
    while True:
        try:
            with httpx.Client() as client:
                with connect_sse(client, 'GET', 'https://stream.wikimedia.
```

```
org/v2/stream/recentchange') as event_source:
                    for item in event_source.iter_sse():
                        vals.put(json.loads(item.data), block=False)
                        await trio.sleep(1)
        except queue.Full:
            print("Queue is full")
            return True


async def monitor():
    while True:
        curr_len = vals.qsize()
        if curr_len >= max_vals:
            fetch_done = True
            return True
        else:
            print("Queue size:",curr_len)
        await trio.sleep(1)


async def serializer():
    while True:
        try:
            item = vals.get_nowait()
            print("item read, Wiki edited by:", item["user"])
            f = trio.Path(f'./tmp/${item["id"]}.json')
            await f.write_text(json.dumps(item))
        except queue.Empty:
            print("Queue is empty")
            if fetch_done == True:
                return True
        await trio.sleep(1)


async def main():
    async with trio.open_nursery() as nursery:
        nursery.start_soon(fetcher)
        nursery.start_soon(monitor)
        nursery.start_soon(serializer)


trio.run(main)
```

The code is basically the same. The coroutines are defined with the async keyword and replacements for helper I/O operation libraries are also available for Trio. The interesting part is the short main coroutine, which, instead of launching the coroutines using the standard asyncio high-level API, opens a nursery and adds the coroutines as tasks inside it.

Here, the nursery acts as a **context manager** for the concurrent tasks. This context manager waits for all child tasks to return a result or raise an exception. In case of an exception in one of them, the context manager notifies the other child tasks to gracefully clean up before being canceled. Once all concurrent tasks are canceled, the exception is propagated back to the parent.

This isolation, notification, and standard exception handling are the basics of the structured concurrency concept. A benefit of this approach is that it prevents threads 'leaking' in tasks, making asynchronous programming safer. Asyncio has incorporated the concept since Python 3.11 as the asyncio.TaskGroup function, which is now the recommended way to create tasks.

Trio has established itself in the Python community. Several companion libraries extend the functionalities for testing, HTTP servers and clients, database client libraries, Internet of Things, command-line user interfaces, and streaming pipelines. It's worth noting that you can support Trio and asyncio simultaneously using one of the several existing wrappers on top of them.

Summary

Asyncio is the standard library for managing cooperative concurrent and asynchronous tasks in Python. It requires that the tasks are awaitable objects (coroutines, futures, or objects that implement the __await__ method). The basic requirement is that the tasks you want to run in asyncio's event loop are non-blocking. If you need it to execute a blocking operation, you have to use Python's multithreading capabilities.

To use asyncio, you have to include the async/await keywords to create coroutines or implement the Awaitable interface and understand the consequences of their interaction. For the most part, you will be able to use asyncio's capabilities without having to manipulate tasks or the event loop directly, but you can access low-level APIs to do so if needs be.

Alternative approaches to implementing highly performant concurrent tasks using asyncio libraries include uvloop, aiofiles, and aiohttp. Otherwise, an alternative way of implementing asynchronous coroutines is to use Trio, which leverages the concept of structured concurrency to make asynchronous programming safer.

In the next two chapters we are going to dig into other details of the asyncio library, to measure the benefits of using it in proper I/O-bound scenarios and to find out how to apply common solutions or patterns to obtain more robust asynchronous solutions.

Get This Book's PDF Version and Exclusive Extras

UNLOCK NOW

Scan the QR code (or go to packtpub.com/unlock). Search for this book by name, confirm the edition, and then follow the steps on the page.

Note: Keep your invoice handy. Purchases made directly from Packt don't require an invoice.

5

Assessing Common Mistakes in Asynchronous Programming

We have established that asynchronous programming doesn't speed up your software solutions all by itself, i.e. your code won't run faster if you apply async/await (or any other asynchronous framework/library construct) on every function. Instead, asynchronous programming makes your code more scalable, **scalability** being a non-functional requirement which means that your solution is able to properly handle increasing demand in terms of users, transactions or data.

Gains in scalability might be reflected in better overall performance, an analogy being a pizza restaurant that has only one oven. If each pizza requires ten minutes to be baked, then in a line of five people the last person will have to wait 50 minutes to get their order. If you scale up the capacity of the oven to three compartments, however, all customers will be served within 20 minutes. You have an overall gain in performance even if each individual transaction is not optimized.

To illustrate our point about performance and scalability, we are going to implement a service that is I/O-intensive, and then walk through the performance gains that result from using coroutines and asynchronous coding changes in our solution. Finally, we will explore how to handle exceptions in coroutines so as to increase our control over their execution.

These are the topics we'll be covering:

- Profiling CPU usage in asynchronous code
- Detecting common mistakes in asynchronous code
- Handling exceptions in asynchronous code

Our use case will be simple: we want to gather information about 200 characters from a well-known TV series (https://en.wikipedia.org/wiki/My_Little_Pony) as fast as possible using a public REST API (https://ponyapi.net/). Each character has many attributes, but we will focus on gathering their name, occupation and classification. The concepts we will be using for this literally toy case will apply equally well to any externally provided resources, such as shared file systems, databases, etc.

Technical requirements

This chapter relies on external public services, and the source code for the examples is available at https://github.com/PacktPublishing/Asynchronous-Programming-in-Python/tree/main/Chapter05. Besides the source code you will find a requirements.txt file containing dependencies that can be installed using pip.

```
$ python3 -m venv .env
$ source .env/bin/activate
$ pip install -r requirements.txt
```

You can substitute the external service dependency by using a local service that mocks the responses, such as MockServer (https://www.mock-server.com/), Prism (https://docs.stoplight.io/docs/prism), or any similar tool.

Profiling CPU usage in asynchronous code

In *Chapter 3* we used a **profiler** to obtain information about resource usage from a multithreaded Python script. In asynchronous contexts deterministic profilers (like the standard cProfile) are not useful because they don't take into account the waiting time. In addition to the previously mentioned py-spy, there is another open-source tool called **Scalene** that is useful for measuring CPU, memory and even GPU usage.

We are going to use the **command line interface (CLI)** provided by Scalene (see https://www.python4data.science/en/24.3.0/performance/scalene.html for information about the CLI options), but there is also a web interface and the programmatic API which allows profile-specific functions/methods to be invoked using the @profile annotation. Scalene provides information about specific lines of code that use CPU/GPU and memory resources. For CPU, Scalene provides three measures of usage as a percentage of the total time: first, the time spent executing python code; second, the time used to execute native code (like C linked libraries); and third, the system time (which includes the I/O waiting time). These features are shown in *Figure 5.1*:

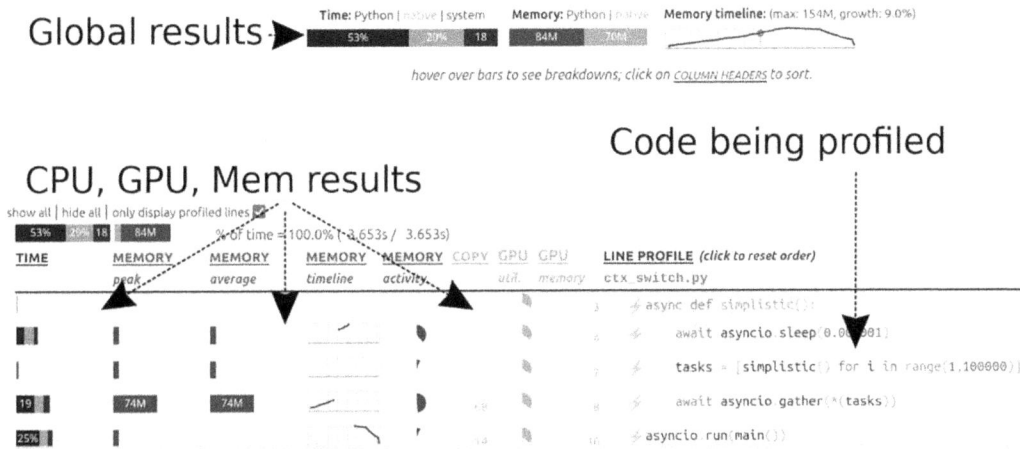

Figure 5.1: Scalene profiling example results

Finally, to provide an enhanced dev experience Scalene also provides a plugin for integration into the well-known **VSCode** (https://vscodium.com/) development environment. This way you can have a complete set of tools – editor, debugger, profiler, AI assistant – to work with your Python scripts.

Detecting common mistakes in asynchronous code

The first implementation of our sample service will show the first and most common mistake of asynchronous implementations: the mixing of blocking and non-blocking code, which the example (available at Chapter 5/extractor_async1.py) makes explicit.

```
import time
import asyncio
import requests
BASE_URL = "https://ponyapi.net/v1/character/"
def get_data(person):
    try:
        p = person["data"][0]
        return f'{p["id"]}, {p["name"]}, {p["occupation"]}, {[k for k in
p["kind"]]}'        except Exception as e:
        return f'Error: {e}'

async def get_data_blocking(url):
    response = requests.get(url, timeout=30)
```

```
    if response.status_code == 200 and len(response.text) > 0:
        return response.json()
    else:
        return None

async def get_people():
    for i in range(1, 200):
        person_data = await get_data_blocking(BASE_URL + str(i))
    print(get_data(person_data))

async def main():
    await get_people()

if name == "main":
    start = time.time()
    asyncio.run(main())
    end = time.time()
    print('Time elapsed:',(end-start),'seconds')
```

The get_people function waits for the get_blocking_data coroutine, which uses the public API to get data from an external service, and it also uses the get_data function to format the results obtained before. The use of coroutines and normal functions is not the core issue with this implementation: the real problem is the mixing of synchronous and asynchronous coding styles, which becomes clear when you use the profiler to check the code (*Figure 5.2*):

```
extractor_async1.py: % of time =  99.99% (2m:55.452s) out of 2m:55.463s.
```

Line	Time Python	native	system	extractor_async1.py
15				async def get_data_blocking(url):
16	3%		97%	response = requests.get(url, timeout=30)

Figure 5.2: Blocking code in asynchronous context

Notice that the Scalene CLI provides the global 'wall time' of execution, along with the code and three other columns. These show the percentage of time used for Python script execution (line 16 uses 3% of the total time executing the code), native (non-Python code) execution, and system time. Most (97%) of the total time is used waiting for the requests library to connect to an external HTTP service execution; the method used from this library is buried behind all the asynchronous function calling.

In the example it is obvious that the purpose of applying asynchronous programming is completely wasted, but in certain cases it is not so easy to detect that an I/O-intensive operation is being wrapped around asynchronous calls. Data operations are a good candidate for special attention, given that data transfer, data storage or database persistence are usually costly in terms of not only execution time but also money. In *Chapter 8* and *Chapter 9* we will dive deep into how you can use asynchronous programming to deliver non-blocking operations of that type.

This blocking operation is easily solved by relaying in one of the most used asynchronous HTTP clients, aiohttp, which provides a non-blocking HTTP connection pooling mechanism to reuse a connection to a server. This way, the overall performance of the solution is greatly improved but also individual request time is reduced by the elimination of some of the connection steps. The updated code (available at `Chapter 5/extractor_async2.py`) shows an alternative implementation using a non-blocking `get_data_nonblocking` coroutine:

```
...
import aiohttp
async def get_data_nonblocking(session, url):
    try:
        async with session.get(url) as resp:
            results = await resp.json()
            return results
    except aiohttp.ClientResponseError as e:
        return str(e)
async def get_people():
    async with aiohttp.ClientSession() as session:
        for i in range(1, 200):
            person_data = await get_data_nonblocking(session,BASE_URL +
str(i))
            print(get_data(person_data))
...
```

This solution reuses a shared `aiohttp.ClientSession()` instance to send the request and process results from the external web service. Benefits of the change are easily visible in *Figure 5.3*, which shows the result of profiling the updated version of the scraper. We see that it now takes 40 seconds to run instead of 2 minutes:

```
extractor_async2.py: % of time = 100.00% (39.467s) out of 39.467s.
```

Line	Time Python	native	system	extractor_async2.py
31				`if __name__ == "__main__":`
32	3%		96%	`    asyncio.run(main())`
33				

Figure 5.3: Non-blocking HTTP data extraction

Although this version is better, the system time still is high (96%), which points to another mistake common in asynchronous implementations: launching several coroutines in a sequential way. The loop of the get_people coroutine works like a sequential implementation because each coroutine starts only after the previous one has been completed. A simple solution for this kind of situation is shown in the following implementation (available at `Chapter 5/extractor_async3.py`):

```
...
async def get_people():
    async with aiohttp.ClientSession() as session:
        tasks = [] for i in range(1, 200):
tasks.append(asyncio.create_task(get_data_nonblocking(session, BASE_URL +
str(i))))
results = await asyncio.gather(*tasks)
    for r in results:
        print(get_data(r))
...
```

The change is subtle but decisive. Instead of iterating over a loop, we use the asyncio.create_task method to wrap the calls to get_data_nonblocking as tasks (which is a type of awaitable if you recall from *Chapter 4*). Those tasks are launched concurrently and awaited using the asyncio. gather method which unpacks the results iterable using the * operator. (You can find the rationale behind this operator in https://peps.python.org/pep-3132/). *Figure 5.4* shows the performance gains delivered by this approach:

```
extractor_async3.py: % of time = 100.00% (8.114s) out of 8.114s.
```

Line	Time Python	native	system	extractor_async3.py
35				if __name__ == "__main__":
36	3%		94%	asyncio.run(main())
37				

Figure 5.4: Non-blocking concurrent extraction

It's worth noticing that these changes have a direct impact on overall performance, improving it more than fivefold, and notice too that the time spent executing Python code has increased to 3% of the total time, while the system time has been reduced to 94%. Notice also that the change in the way the results are printed (batch vs. on-the-fly) adds some latency too.

The concurrent execution of tasks is a great tool with which to take advantage of asynchronous programming, but if you split a workload into multiple micro-tasks you may incur a penalty due to event loop context switching. The following code (available at Chapter 5/ctx_switch.py) creates a large number of tasks that do nothing apart from wait a fraction of a second:

```python
import asyncio

async def simplistic():
    await asyncio.sleep(0.000001)

async def main():
    tasks = [simplistic() for i in range(1,100000)]
    await asyncio.gather(*(tasks))

asyncio.run(main())
```

Figure 5.5 shows the results of profiling this code – notice that Scalene gives a good estimate of memory usage. (We have omitted the CPU measurement this time for brevity.)

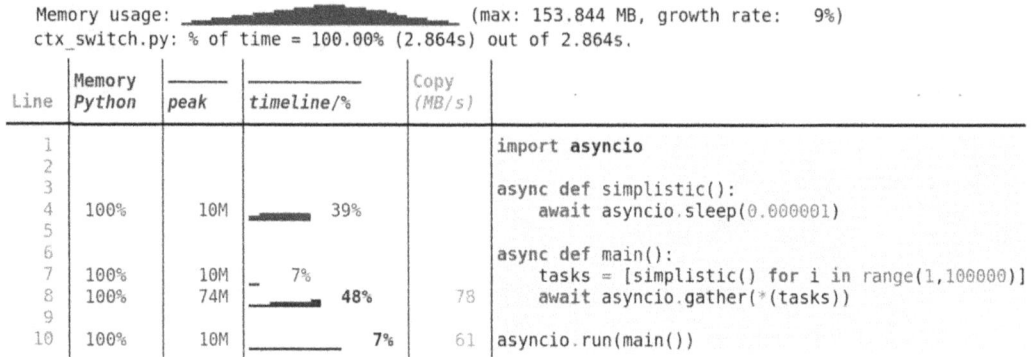

```
Memory usage: ▁▃▅▆▆▅▄▃▂ (max: 153.844 MB, growth rate:   9%)
ctx_switch.py: % of time = 100.00% (2.864s) out of 2.864s.
```

Line	Memory Python	peak	timeline/%	Copy (MB/s)	
1					`import asyncio`
2					
3					`async def simplistic():`
4	100%	10M	▄▄▄ 39%		`    await asyncio.sleep(0.000001)`
5					
6					`async def main():`
7	100%	10M	▁ 7%		`    tasks = [simplistic() for i in range(1,100000)]`
8	100%	74M	▁▄▄▄ 48%	78	`    await asyncio.gather(*(tasks))`
9					
10	100%	10M	▁▁▁▁ 7%	61	`asyncio.run(main())`

Figure 5.5: Performance penalization by excessive context switching

In this case we have used Scalene to measure not only the CPU/GPU time, but also the memory involved. The principal concern is that the `asyncio.gather()` method is the most expensive one: we can see that the memory used to gather the results of the tasks is seven times the memory required to execute them. This means that the tasks involved aren't good candidates for aggressive splitting, since the context switching between tasks is more costly than the possible benefits. Going back to our previous example, there are other important aspects to consider in relation to implementation robustness: **exception handling** and **error logging**.

Handling exceptions in asynchronous code

The basic rules of Python exception handling in asynchronous code are identical to those which apply to synchronous implementations, but you must decide whether to handle exceptions locally in the coroutine/task or propagate them up to the caller.

In previous implementations you can see that a really generic behavior is implemented in the `get_data_nonblocking` method: if a `aiohttp.ClientResponseError` is thrown then the result is a string with the message of the error. This breaks the method contract (a `dict` is expected as result) and the returned message is uninformative. Similarly, the get_data method handles all possible exceptions by just returning them as a string, which is also not the best way to report the anomaly. The following code (available at `Chapter 5/extractor_async4.py`) shows an alternative implementation which offers some improvements:

```python
import asyncio
import aiohttp

BASE_URL = https://ponyapi.net/v1/character/

def get_data(person):
    try: p = person["data"][0]
        return f'{p["id"]}, {p["name"]}, {p["occupation"]}, {[k for k in
p["kind"]]}'
    except (KeyError, IndexError) as e:
        return f'Error processing data: {e}'
    except Exception as e:
        return f'Unexpected error: {e}'

async def fetch_person(session, url):
    try:
        async with session.get(url) as resp:
            if resp.status == 200:
                return await resp.json()
            else:
                return f"Error: Status code {resp.status} for {url}"
    except aiohttp.ClientError as e:
        return f"Client error: {e} for {url}"
    except asyncio.TimeoutError:
        return f"Timeout error for {url}"

async def get_people():
    async with aiohttp.ClientSession() as session:
        tasks = [fetch_person(session, BASE_URL + str(i)) for i in
range(1, 200)]
        results = await asyncio.gather(*tasks, return_exceptions=True)
        for result in results:
            print(get_data(result) if isinstance(result, dict) else
result)
```

The changes are a compromise between local coroutine try/except statements and the caller's asyncio parameters. At coroutine level, specific errors have been included in the function, but the same behavior of changing the result type in case of error remains. To handle this as a feature and not a bug we use the asyncio.gather return_exceptions parameter, to make sure that exceptions raised by individual tasks are included in the result list. This way, using the isinstance method we can determine whether a dictionary is returned and then either process the result or just print it as an error log.

The default behavior of the asyncio.gather method (i.e. without setting return_exceptions to true) is to wrap any exception thrown by a task into another exception and cancel any remaining awaited tasks. Individual awaited tasks that have thrown an exception can be inspected using the task.exception() method; this will return the actual error which occurred while running the task.

Every error should be logged properly to help debugging, but (as we previously discussed) logging is also an I/O-intensive task which should be written in a non-blocking way so as to avoid expending valuable thread time on a support task. In our example the get_data function writes messages to standard output in case of an error, which might have an impact on overall performance if there are many such errors. An updated version of the code (available at Chapter 5/extractor_async5.py) with asynchronous logging management looks like this:

```python
import queue
import asyncio
import logging
from logging.handlers import QueueHandler, QueueListener
import aiohttp


log_queue = queue.Queue()
queue_handler = QueueHandler(log_queue)
listener = QueueListener(log_queue, *logging.root.handlers)
logging.root.addHandler(queue_handler)
listener.start()
logger = logging.getLogger(__name__)
BASE_URL = "https://ponyapi.net/v1/character/"

def print_data(person):
    try:
        p = person["data"][0]
        print(f'{p["id"]}, {p["name"]}, {p["occupation"]}, {[k for k in
```

```
    p["kind"]]}')
        except (KeyError, IndexError) as e:
            logger.error('Error processing data: %s',e)
        except Exception as e:
            logger.error('Unexpected error: %s',e)


async def fetch_person(session, url):
    try:
        async with session.get(url) as resp:
            return await resp.json() if resp.status == 200 else f"Error in
HTTP client for {url}"
    except aiohttp.ClientError as e:
        logger.error("Client error: %s for %s", e, url)
    except asyncio.TimeoutError:
        logger.error("Timeout error for %s", e)
    return None



async def get_people():
    async with aiohttp.ClientSession() as session:
        tasks = [fetch_person(session, BASE_URL + str(i)) for i in
range(1, 200)]

        results = await asyncio.gather(*tasks, return_exceptions=True)

        for result in results:
            if isinstance(result, dict):
                print_data(result)
    ...
```

This implementation uses the logging module's QueueHandler and QueueListener classes to separate the execution thread from the logging thread. A target queue is created and the QueueHandler instance will listen to the logging messages and put them into that queue. Similarly, the QueueListener is responsible for consuming messages that are pending in the queue and for dispatching them to configured logging handlers. This way you can send the messages to external services or write them to local storage without blocking the task that generated the messages, as a result of which you may also notice a small improvement in the global execution time.

Summary

In this chapter we have navigated through some of the most common implementation errors that can be incurred when you use asynchronous programming with the standard asyncio library. These errors can have a direct impact on the performance of your solutions and serve to remind us that asynchronous programming doesn't invariably imply better performance instantly. To summarize the practices presented in this chapter:

- Do not mix blocking code inside asynchronous coroutines/tasks
- Avoid waiting for one coroutine or task to finish before launching another
- Favor launching enough tasks concurrently to maximize the usage of the underlying resources
- Do not launch a huge number of small tasks, to avoid incurring unnecessary context switching between them
- Apply consistent management of exceptions inside the coroutines/tasks and proper handling of exceptions in parent threads
- Separate logging tasks from the main execution thread to maximize the throughput of your solutions

In the next chapter we will move on to some useful asynchronous patterns that should help you to plan and design asynchronous solutions for a variety of business contexts.

6

Testing and Asynchronous Design Patterns

In the previous chapter we discussed some of the practices you want to avoid in order to obtain a performant asynchronous solution. Now our focus changes, as we explore some standard ways of solving typical problems. When you identify similar scenarios in your own context you'll be able to adapt the code to cover your needs.

With the emergence of new use cases comes a growing number of software development patterns. For example, the current artificial intelligence (AI) wave is bringing new challenges related to adoption of the new technologies, for which new patterns may be appropriate, while other patterns are falling out of favor because of the changing software environment. The patterns selected here are by no means exhaustive but they cover the situations that commonly arise in many asynchronous implementations.

We will start the chapter with a summary of **testing asynchronous code**, given that previously we have profiled the code to gain insight into its behavior, and because coding with neither testing nor visibility is a clear anti-pattern in many cases.

In this chapter we're going to cover the following topics:

- Testing and debugging asynchronous code
- Working with the half-synchronous/half-asynchronous pattern
- Implementing the monitor object pattern
- Using the read-write lock pattern
- Applying the leader/followers pattern

For each pattern we will include some common rules of thumb for spotting the use cases to which they apply, and some advice about the benefits you can expect when you include them as part of your solution.

Technical requirements

For this chapter, we will use some external packages to extend the basic asyncio library. First, we will use **pytest** as a testing library, along with a couple of extensions (pytest-asyncio and pytest-xdist) to run tests for asyncio and also be able to run them in parallel. Of course, the same concepts apply for any other library (e.g. the standard module unittest). Then instead of consuming actual external resources we will mock responses using aioresponse. As usual, all the source code is available in the Github repository, in the Chapter06 folder (https://github. com/PacktPublishing/Asynchronous-Programming-in-Python). Remember to generate a virtual environment exclusively for the chapter. That way, the additional packages will not interfere with other requirements:

```
$ python3 -m venv .venv
$ source .venv/bin/activate
$ pip install -r requirements.txt
```

Testing asynchronous code

Our first example will show two tasks that are going to run concurrently. One will extract some data from the Nobel Prize laureates REST API and the other will simulate a printing job for documents (source code available at Chapter 6/concurrent_tasks.py):

```python
import asyncio
import aiohttp


URL = "https://api.nobelprize.org/2.1/laureate/"


async def get_nobel_facts(nid):
    print("Starting nobel extraction")
    await asyncio.sleep(5)
    async with aiohttp.ClientSession() as session:
        async with session.get(URL + str(nid)) as response:
            if response.status == 200:
                nobel = await response.json()
```

```
                    print(nobel[0]["knownName"]["en"])



async def print_document(doc_name, sleep_time):
    print(f"[{time.strftime('%X')}] Print '{doc_name}'...")
    await asyncio.sleep(sleep_time)
    print(f"[{time.strftime('%X')}] Finished.")



async def main():
    await asyncio.gather(get_nobel_name(659), get_odds(10))
```

To test the code, we create a script that uses the pytest fixtures to check tasks' individual results (source code available at Chapter 6/test1.py):

```
import pytest
import pytest_asyncio
import concurrent_tasks


@pytest_asyncio.fixture
async def nobel_name():
    return "Gabriel García Márquez"


@pytest.mark.asyncio
async def test_get_nobel_name(nobel_name):
    result = await concurrent_tasks.get_nobel_name(659)
    assert result == nobel_name


@pytest.mark.asyncio
async def test_print_docs():
    start_time = time.perf_counter()
    doc1 = concurrent_tasks.print_document("long", 3)
    doc2 = concurrent_tasks.print_document("short", 1)
    doc3 = concurrent_tasks.print_document("med", 2)
    await asyncio.gather(doc1, doc2, doc3)
    end_time = time.perf_counter()
    duration = end_time - start_time
    assert duration == pytest.approx(3.0, abs=0.1)
```

Notice that the test uses **fixtures** in the assertions instead of method-level constants, meaning that you can reuse them across several tests cleanly, while the use of `pytest.mark.asyncio` annotation to mark a coroutine as a test case allows you to await asynchronous functions in a natural way. You can control the lifecycle of the event loop used by fixtures using the `asyncio_default_fixture_loop_scope` in the pytest config file or by a CLI call. Essentially, it determines when the event loop is created and destroyed.

In the test for the dummy `print_document` function we use an assertion in the `test_print_docs` function to check that the three documents were printed concurrently. Given that the duration of the task is set as an argument for the `print_document` function and the longest task takes three seconds to complete, the duration of the test should be closer to three seconds instead of six (which would be the duration if the three documents were not printed concurrently).

You can run the test cases using the CLI:

```
$ python -m pytest test1.py
```

This test runs against actual external resources, and this can be problematic in some situations, for example if the external resource has a usage rate limit or if it is slow and you want to test functionality instead of performance. In those cases you can replace the call to the actual resource by a **mock** that responds instantly with the expected contract. In the following example we include a mock response from the Nobel API in the test case to avoid using the actual API (source code available at `Chapter 6/test2.py`):

```python
import pytest
import pytest_asyncio
import concurrent_tasks
from aioresponses import aioresponses

@pytest_asyncio.fixture
def mock_aioresponse():
    with aioresponses() as m:
        yield m

@pytest.mark.asyncio
async def test_get_nobel_name(nobel_name, mock_aioresponse):
    data=[{"knownName": {"en":"Gabriel García Márquez"}}]
    mock_aioresponse.get( "https://api.nobelprize.org/2.1/laureate/659",
payload=data )
```

```
        result = await concurrent_tasks.get_nobel_name(659)
        assert result == nobel_name
```

This time a new fixture solving the expected response from the external resource is used in the test_get_nobel_name test coroutine. Mocks are a common way to isolate testing, but they should be used carefully given that there might be hidden API contract changes, and further effort may be required to generate mocks for more complex scenarios. All other good practices about testing are applicable to asynchronous testing, including parameterization, parallelization, grouping and idempotency. A great resource for information about testing with pytest for several use cases is available at https://pytest-with-eric.com/. Now that we can test our solutions let's move on to writing some patterns to solve common problems in asynchronous programming.

Working with the half-synchronous/half-asynchronous pattern

One of the main anti-patterns we discussed in the previous chapter was the mix of synchronous calls into asynchronous code, but more often than not you will have CPU-intensive workloads mixed with I/O-intensive operations. In such cases, enabling both worlds to work together instead of colliding is an incredibly useful capability, which the **half-sync/half-async pattern** delivers by delegating tasks that might block the main thread to an external executor thread. The following code (available at Chapter 6/half_sync.py) shows a simple implementation:

```python
import asyncio
import concurrent.futures


async def cpu_bound_task(x):
    await asyncio.sleep(1)
    return x * x


def run_cpu_bound_task(x):
    return asyncio.run(cpu_bound_task(x))


async def main():
    with concurrent.futures.ThreadPoolExecutor() as pool:
        loop = asyncio.get_running_loop()
        tasks = [
            loop.run_in_executor(pool, run_cpu_bound_task, i)
            for i in range(5)
```

```
        ]
        results = await asyncio.gather(*tasks)
        print(results)

if name == "main":
    asyncio.run(main())
```

A coroutine that is CPU-expensive (matrix multiplication, machine learning model inference, etc.) defined in the `cpu_bound_task` function might usually block the `event_loop`, but instead of being scheduled in the main thread, we declare a context with the `concurrent.futures.ThreadPoolExecutor()`. This will be used to launch each task in a separate thread (using the `run_in_executor` method of the running loop), so that the main thread is not blocked but the `asyncio.gather` can get all awaited results. The key feature is the `run_cpu_bound_task` function, which is a wrapper for the asynchronous coroutine.

In other implementations you can use a queue to pass messages from the synchronous results to be postprocessed by I/O-intensive asynchronous code. This pattern can lead to performance improvements by offloading long running tasks into separate threads while keeping the main execution thread responsive for new tasks.

Implementing the monitor object pattern

Another important topic in asynchronous programming is access to shared resources. When you work synchronously the access is sequential and traceable, but the gains in efficiency and scalability that asynchronous solutions provide mean that certain resources are more susceptible to race conditions that might lead to incorrect results. In these cases, access to shared resources can be controlled by putting a mutual exclusion mechanism in place that allows only one coroutine to perform operations over the resource, or even better a set of conditions to determine when a coroutine is allowed to access the resource.

In the following example (available at `Chapter 6/monitor_queue.py`) a bounded queue is used to represent shared resources that have a hard limit on capacity, two **producers** that act as clients have several tasks to be operated through the shared resources, and two customers act as operators that free up the resources:

```
import queue
import random
import asyncio
```

```
class MonitorQueue:
    def init(self, maxsize=3):
        self._queue = queue.Queue(maxsize=maxsize)
        self._lock = asyncio.Lock()
        self._not_empty = asyncio.Condition(self._lock)
        self._not_full = asyncio.Condition(self._lock)

    async def enqueue(self, item):
        async with self._lock:
            while self._queue.full():
                await self._not_full.wait()
            self._queue.put(item)
            self._not_empty.notify_all()
            print(f"Enqueued: {item}, size: {self._queue.qsize()}")

    async def dequeue(self):
        async with self._lock:
            while self._queue.empty():
                await self._not_empty.wait()
            item = self._queue.get()
            self._not_full.notify_all()
            print(f"Dequeued: {item}")
            return item
```

The MonitorQueue class wraps the shared resource and provides two methods, enqueue and dequeue, as an interface to apply operations over that resource in an asynchronous way. The asyncio.Lock() call provides a mechanism to mutually exclude tasks from access to the underlying queue operations. The _not_full and _not_empty conditions work as flags to add/remove items from the queue, preventing the queue.Empty and queue.Full exceptions from being raised when illegal operations are attempted on the queue. The same mechanism can be implemented to throttle calls to external APIs or to use filesystem capabilities. The following code shows how to use the class with concurrent producers/consumers:

```
async def producer(monitor_queue, producer_id):
    for i in range(10):
        item = f"Producer {producer_id} - Item {i}"
```

```
            await monitor_queue.enqueue(item)
            await asyncio.sleep(random.random() * 0.5)


async def consumer(monitor_queue, consumer_id):
    while True:
        item = await monitor_queue.dequeue()
        print(f"Consumer - {consumer_id} - Got {item}")
        await asyncio.sleep(random.random() * 1)


async def main():
    monitor_queue = MonitorQueue()
    producer1 = asyncio.create_task(producer(monitor_queue, 1))
    producer2 = asyncio.create_task(producer(monitor_queue, 2))
    consumer1 = asyncio.create_task(consumer(monitor_queue, 1))
    consumer2 = asyncio.create_task(consumer(monitor_queue, 2))

    await asyncio.gather(producer1, producer2)
    await asyncio.sleep(5)
    consumer1.cancel()
    consumer2.cancel()

    try:
        await consumer1
    except asyncio.CancelledError:
        print("Consumer 1 cancelled")
    try:
        await consumer2
    except asyncio.CancelledError:
        print("Consumer 2 cancelled")
```

Two concurrent producers are launched and awaited, and each one makes use of the shared monitored resource and waits until the **consumers** have free space in the queue to complete their operations. Notice how consumers are canceled before being awaited, and consumers are still running while the signal is sent, so therefore we have to handle the cancellation exception once the task is effectively cancelled.

This pattern – referred to as the **monitor object pattern** – might not improve the overall performance of a solution, but it encapsulates the resource usage and provides a mechanism to minimize the overload of shared resources, bringing robustness to your code.

Using the read-write lock pattern

Some use cases are biased towards read operations rather than write ones, for example in cache systems in which the number of reads over a piece of data is expected to be several orders of magnitude higher than the number of writes. In such cases the **read-write lock pattern** is handy because it allows concurrent reads over the shared resource and single-operation access for writing. The following example (available at Chapter 6/read_write.py) shows a simple implementation based on an enumeration to control the possible states of shared resource, and privileging write access over read access:

```python
import asyncio
from enum import Enum

class LockState(Enum):
    IDLE = 0
    READING = 1
    WRITING = 2

class AsyncReadWriteLock:
    def init(self):
        self._state = LockState.IDLE
        self._reader_count = 0
        self._writer_waiting = 0
        self._condition = asyncio.Condition()

    async def read_acquire(self):
        async with self._condition:
            while self._state == LockState.WRITING or self._writer_waiting
> 0:
                await self._condition.wait()
            self._reader_count += 1
            self._state = LockState.READING

    async def read_release(self):
        async with self._condition:
            self._reader_count -= 1
            if self._reader_count == 0:
                self._state = LockState.IDLE
```

```
                    self._condition.notify_all()

        async def write_acquire(self):
            async with self._condition:
                self._writer_waiting += 1
                while self._state != LockState.IDLE:
                    await self._condition.wait()
                self._writer_waiting -= 1
                self._state = LockState.WRITING

        async def write_release(self):
            async with self._condition:
                self._state = LockState.IDLE
                self._condition.notify_all()
```

The class includes methods to acquire writer/reader locks based on the state of the resource. Notice the double wait condition in the read_acquire method: if the resource is being written to, or if there is at least one writer waiting, the reader keeps waiting. This is the bias towards writers that we mentioned before. The following code shows a sample client that launches readers and writers to run concurrently:

```
async def reader(lock, id):
    await lock.read_acquire()
    print(f"Reader {id} acquired read lock")
    await asyncio.sleep(0.1)
    print(f"Reader {id} releasing read lock")
    await lock.read_release()

async def writer(lock, id):
    await lock.write_acquire()
    print(f"Writer {id} acquired write lock")
    await asyncio.sleep(0.2)
    print(f"Writer {id} releasing write lock")
    await lock.write_release()

async def main():
    lock = AsyncReadWriteLock()
```

```
    tasks = [ reader(lock, 1), reader(lock, 2), writer(lock, 1),
reader(lock, 3), writer(lock, 2), reader(lock, 4), reader(lock, 5), ]
    await asyncio.gather(*tasks)

if name == "main":
    asyncio.run(main())
```

The reader/writer functions create clients that operate over the read-write lock instance, simu-lating long operations. The output shows you that readers are on hold while writers finish their work, but once the lock is free all readers work concurrently:

```
There are 1 readers
Reader 1 acquired read lock
There are 2 readers
Reader 2 acquired read lock
Reader 1 releasing read lock
Reader 2 releasing read lock
Writer 1 acquired write lock
Writer 1 releasing write lock
Writer 2 acquired write lock
Writer 2 releasing write lock
There are 1 readers
Reader 3 acquired read lock
There are 2 readers
Reader 4 acquired read lock
There are 3 readers
Reader 5 acquired read lock
Reader 3 releasing read lock
Reader 4 releasing read lock
Reader 5 releasing read lock
```

The read-write lock pattern makes sense when you want to maintain consistency in particular data structures like graphs or trees, in which it is preferable to keep reads waiting until the mod-ifications are spread completely across the data.

Applying the leader/followers pattern

When you have a stream of tasks the **leader/followers pattern** can be useful as a way of encapsulating task generation/execution responsibilities into different components. A common scenario in which this pattern is applied involves multithreaded web servers in which the leader process sets up a pool of worker threads waiting to handle concurrent requests. As we will explore in the next chapter, this model can be scaled out using entirely asynchronous implementation of the web servers.

The idea is that a leader takes incoming task requests and assigns the actual operation to workers from a pool, as shown in the following example (available at `Chapter 6/leader-follower.py`) of a simple single-node implementation of the pattern:

```python
import asyncio
import random

async def worker(queue, worker_id):
    while True:
        task = await queue.get()
        if task is None:
            queue.task_done()
            break
        print(f"Worker {worker_id} processing task: {task}")
        await asyncio.sleep( random.uniform(0.1, 0.5))
        print(f"Worker {worker_id} finished task: {task}")
        queue.task_done()

async def leader(queue, num_tasks, num_workers):
    for i in range(num_tasks):
        task = f"Task {i + 1}"
        await queue.put(task)
        print(f"Leader added task: {task}")
        await asyncio.sleep(random.uniform(0.2, 0.8))
    for _ in range(num_workers):
        await queue.put(None)
    await queue.join()

async def main():
```

```
    num_workers = 3
    num_tasks = 10
    queue = asyncio.Queue()
    workers = [asyncio.create_task(worker(queue, i)) for i in range(num_
workers)]
    await leader(queue, num_tasks, num_workers)
    await asyncio.gather(*workers)
```

In this case the leader enqueues all pending tasks and then adds a None task to send a sign to all workers to stop consuming tasks from the queue. This approach works for a bounded set of tasks, but it is usually implemented in conjunction with the monitor pattern that we discussed before to process streams of data when a limited number of workers are available.

Summary

In this chapter we have walked through some of the concurrency patterns that are useful for handling common situations in asynchronous programming. Each pattern can help to maintain code that adheres to the **single responsibility principle** (check https://realpython.com/solid-principles-python/ for more information about SOLID principles).

A good test suite for asynchronous code doesn't guarantee perfection, but does allow you to detect edge cases and possible race conditions. The unittest library included in standard Python is a good example that supports asynchronous mocking and fixtures, but other community-maintained libraries such as pytest can also help with testing complex scenarios.

In the next chapter we explore how asynchronous programming has been included in some of the most popular web frameworks in the Python ecosystem, some of which have evolved to support asynchronous programming while others have been asynchronous-native right from the start.

7

Asynchronous Programming in Django, Flask and Quart

Python frameworks are a common starting point for Python developers, the ubiquity and large community support for many of them creating a good place to adopt language enhancements and best practices. In this chapter we will review three different Python frameworks and their support for asynchronous programming.

The chapter starts with a brief review of the **Model-View-Controller (MVC)** pattern. This established a de facto standard approach to solving many early Web problems, and MVC proved itself as a starter kit for delivering Create-Read-Update-Delete (CRUD) applications. The pattern merits discussion here because many of the most popular frameworks in the Python ecosystem implement their own versions of it. Other frameworks are more agnostic and let you implement other patterns, but maintain the availability of asynchronous programming mechanisms, even if their use is not enforced.

Several Python frameworks became popular way before asynchronous programming mechanisms had become incorporated into Python's core APIs. The inclusion of asynchronous programming support opened a new chapter for many frameworks, because the implications for the frameworks' underlying design decisions were far-reaching and had to be addressed in a consistent way. Frameworks like **Django** and **Flask** evolved to be hybrid in nature, supporting both synchronous and asynchronous programming paradigms to differing degrees, while lately we've seen new asynchronous-native frameworks like **FastAPI**, **Quart** and **Litestar** embracing the new capabilities of asynchronous programming but requiring a shift in how developers think about CRUD, transactions, data modeling, testing and deployment.

Knowledge of how Python frameworks support asynchronous programming always comes in handy when architecting solutions, given the challenges that exist around migrating from one paradigm to the other, or mixing the two.

In this chapter, therefore, we'll be looking at the following topics:

- The Model-View-Controller pattern
- Asynchronous capabilities in Flask
- Quart: a fully asynchronous web framework
- Django asynchronous support

Technical requirements

We will use the base installation package for each of the frameworks we investigate. We have implemented the examples in isolated environments so you will need a different `requirements.txt` file for each framework (`https://github.com/PacktPublishing/Asynchronous-Programming-in-Python`). Remember to generate a virtual environment exclusively for the chapter. That way, the additional packages will not interfere with other requirements:

```
$ python -m venv .venv
$ source .venv/bin/activate
$ pip install -r requirements-flask.txt
```

Reviewing the MVC pattern

The Model-View-Controller is one of the preferred patterns for implementing client/server architectures for the Web. To simplify slightly, its purpose is to segregate responsibilities across three roles:

- **Models** which encapsulate the logic and behavior rules that are not part of the interface of the system (note that interface in this context refers to programming/user interfaces rather than interfaces that define contracts classes must implement);
- **Views** that render domain models or Data Transfer Objects (DTOs) as part of the interface;
- **Controllers** that handle serialization of user input and the creation of views from user actions, and which in Web environments also handle initial requests.

The following diagram shows a simplified version of the pattern:

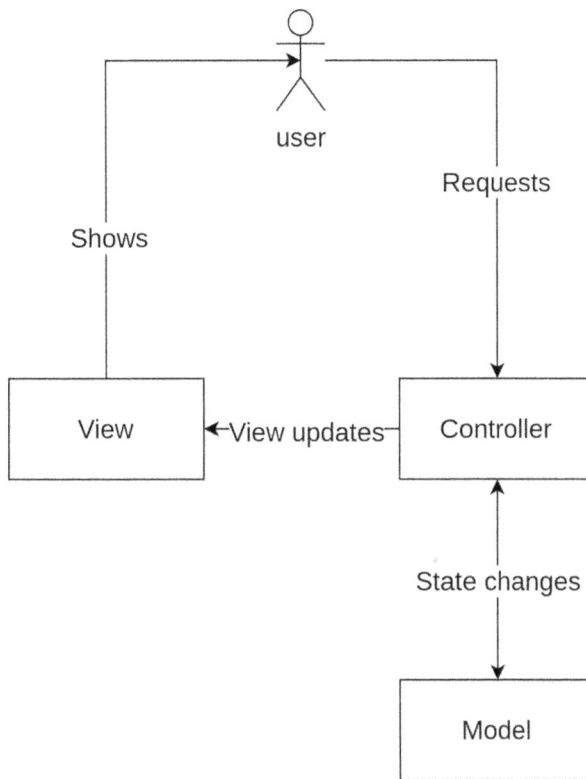

Figure 7.1: MVC pattern

This pattern has many variations. In the Django framework it is recognized as Model-View-Template (MVT), with Django's Views being equivalent to Controllers and Templates to Views, while other variations include the Model-View-View-Model and Model-View-Presenter patterns which are included in other web frameworks.

For the sake of clear discussion, in this chapter we aim to use the MVC nomenclature as standard for all the frameworks presented. If you want to dig deeper into software patterns (and you should!), check out the Catalog of Patterns of Enterprise Application Architecture (https://martinfowler.com/eaaCatalog/) and the Enterprise Integration Patterns site (https://www.enterpriseintegrationpatterns.com/) as valuable seed resources.

Understanding asynchronous capabilities in Flask

Flask is a minimalistic framework in which you can implement your own interpretation of the MVC pattern. The framework is loosely constrained in terms of what you can do, but in its roots Flask is conceived as a **Web Server Gateway Interface (WSGI)** supported application. WSGI defines a standard interface between HTTP and Python, which means that to deploy a Flask-based solution you need a Web server that handles HTTP requests, translates them into Python through WSGI, and then returns the responses back to the client. *Figure 7.2* shows how WSGI applications operate:

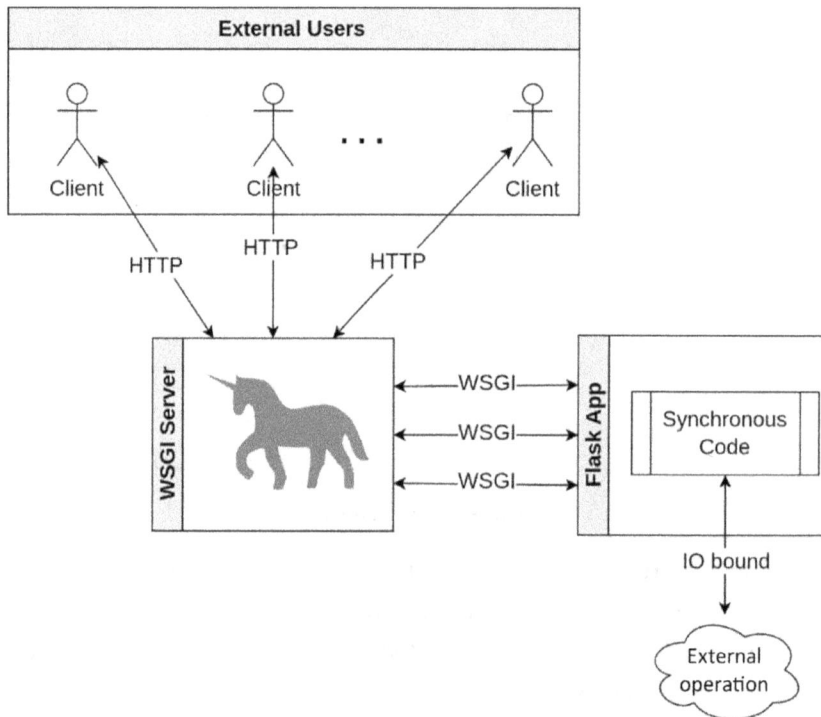

Figure 7.2: WSGI application operation

You will notice that in this schema there are two points at which you can address concurrency in your applications: the web server and the application itself. Interestingly, you can test different approaches to handling concurrency approaches, including asynchronous, in some WSGI servers (like **Gunicorn** https://docs.gunicorn.org/en/stable/) while keeping synchronous code in your Flask application. The following modes are supported:

- **Process**: In sync mode Gunicorn creates an operating system process per worker, so if you configure the number of workers as five you will have six processes – the master plus five workers. This is the default synchronous configuration, which means that each HTTP request will wait until your application returns a response. If you have I/O-bounded tasks such as calls to web services or long-term data access operations, you will be blocking the worker.

- **Threads**: In this case each HTTP request is attached to a green thread inside a worker process, which means that you scale in a $P{\times}T$ relation where P is the number of worker processes and T the number of threads. Again each thread waits until the application returns a response.

- **Greenlets**: This is an asynchronous worker implementation that uses gevent (https://www.gevent.org/) to support the handling of HTTP requests as coroutines. Synchronous applications get some of the benefits of non-blocking coroutine scheduling, plus it will be operating to a scale higher than $P{\times}T$ because the worker thread will not be blocked by each individual request.

Using these three options you can establish a baseline for how asynchronous programming, although not directly codified in your application, could impact your workloads. There is also support for other worker types (eventlet, tornado or even custom worker implementations) that you can explore with minor modifications.

Flask support for asynchronous operations

Beyond support for asynchronous concurrency handling in WSGI servers, Flask evolved to support coroutine-based implementations for many of its features, including *routes*, *error handlers*, *before request*, *after request*, and *teardown* functions. This means that you can use async/await clauses during the handling of WSGI requests, but the code will run synchronously. If you deploy an application which uses asynchronous programming behind a WSGI server, the server will be able to run the code, but it will not be asynchronously executed.

For example, imagine that you want to add observability to a Flask application and send to the telemetry collector a metric each time a request is handled. A simple Flask application could benefit from performing such operations in an asynchronous way, as simulated in the following code (available at Chapter07/flask_wsgi.py):

```
import asyncio
from threading import current_thread
from flask import Flask, jsonify
```

```python
from aiohttp import ClientSession

app = Flask(__name__)
LOGGING_URL = "https://postman-echo.com/post"

async def post_url(data):
    async with ClientSession() as session:
        response = await session.post(LOGGING_URL, data=data)
    return {'url': str(response.url), 'status': response.status,
'data':await response.json()}

@app.before_request
async def app_before_request():
    print(f'Sending message before request: {current_thread().name}')
    await post_url({'message': f'Inside app_before_request(): {current_
thread().name}'})

@app.after_request
async def app_after_request(response):
    print(f'Posting message after response: {response.status}')
    await post_url({'message': f'Returning response status: {response.
status}'})
    return response

@app.errorhandler(404)
async def page_not_found(e):
    print(f'Error caught: {e} in {current_thread().name}')
    results = await post_url(f'Error caught: {e}')
    return jsonify(results), 404

@app.route('/')
async def index():
    print(f'Inside route index(): {current_thread().name}')
    await asyncio.sleep(1)
    return jsonify({"message":"ok"})

if __name__ == '__main__':
    app.run()
```

The first thing you notice is that we are posting all our logging messages to a public echo service provided by a third party. This external service might be slow or unavailable, and being an I/O-bounded type of workload is a good candidate for being implemented using asynchronous programming.

Then it's worth pointing out that if you run the application behind a WSGI server, the execution of the app_before_request, index and app_after_request functions will be executed sequentially, and the I/O-bounded problem of consuming an external service will be no different than if you have it written without the async/await clauses.

Finally, when a route is not available, for example a request to the endpoint /this_endpoint_does_not_exist, the asynchronous error handler posts the error to the external service before returning the error view to the end user. You can run the example using Gunicorn with different worker configurations (notice that you can check that the server is running by connecting an HTTP client, for example curl, or by pointing your browser http://127.0.0.1:8000):

```
$ gunicorn -k sync -w 2 --threads 1 flask_wsgi:app
$ gunicorn -k eventlet --threads 10 flask_wsgi:app
$ gunicorn -k gevent flask_wsgi:app
```

An interesting exercise is to compare the limits of those configurations using a load generator tool like Locust (https://locust.io/).

Asynchronous Server Gateway Interface servers

So, why include the support for async/await in Flask if there is no real gain? The answer: to make Flask compatible with truly asynchronous servers, developed to take advantage of asynchronous programming.

Once the WSGI specification limits were reached, for example when challenges to implementing support for the HTTP/2 spec were encountered, the industry moved to reimplementing the way that asynchronous Python applications could interface HTTP requests. From this work the **Asynchronous Server Gateway Interface (ASGI)** specification was born, extending the support for new protocols besides HTTP 1.1, including Websockets, HTTP/2, and QUIC.

The key change from WSGI to ASGI was the introduction of *events* as the atomic unit of information passed between the web server and the application to communicate different stages and data within a connection. This allowed requests to be segmented in several events that could be handled using asynchronous programming constructs, like coroutines, more efficiently. The following diagram shows how ASGI servers handle events to serve requests in different protocols:

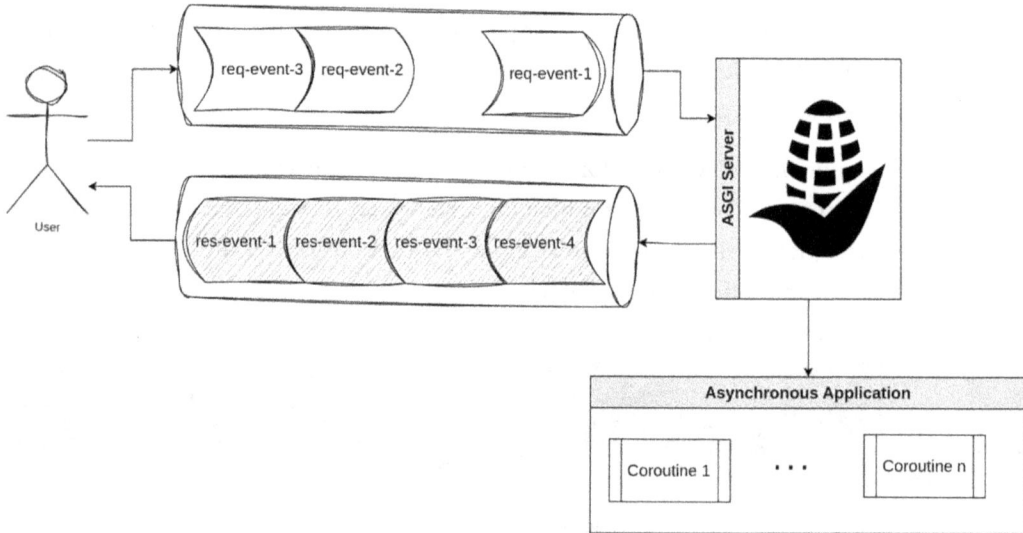

Figure 7.3: ASGI application operation

ASGI is the default interface for asynchronous-native applications, given that non-blocking coroutines are a perfect mechanism for handling concurrent small chunks of requests. Flask apps can use a bridge adapter between WSGI and ASGI called **WsgiToAsgi** (https://github.com/django/asgiref#wsgi-to-asgi-adapter), deployed behind an ASGI server, to obtain some of the advantages of asynchronous programming if the app includes async/await functions (as in our example app).

The WsgiToAsgi bridge does not make your Flask application asynchronous magically; it just allows the ASGI server to run your WSGI app. Modifying our code to be run behind the popular ASGI server Hypercorn (https://github.com/pgjones/hypercorn/) necessitates some small modifications (available at Chapter 7/flask_asgi.py):

```
from asgiref.wsgi import WsgiToAsgi
from flask import Flask

app = Flask(__name__)
```

```
...

asgi_app = WsgiToAsgi(app)
```

Now, if you run the Flask app behind the **Hypercorn** ASGI Server, the benefits of asynchronous I/O operations will be in place for the async implementations of the app_before_request, index and app_after_request functions. The app can consume the external service without blocking the Flask view execution. You can run the application using Hypercorn in a similar way:

```
$ hypercorn flask_asgi:asgi_app
```

Like Gunicorn, Hypercorn has different worker classes that implement the asynchronous supports in different ways. You can rely on the default asyncio (the only one supported by Flask natively), but there are trio and uvloop implementations too that might give you better performance and/ or scalability.

An important caveat is that Flask reuses the event loop provided by the ASGI server in which it is running. Hence when a controller route executes, depending on the ASGI server implementation all unfinished tasks could be cancelled once the controller returns a view to the client, even if they are not finished. For example, in the following code the background task background_process might never be completed:

```
@app.route("/long_running_task")
async def process_data():
    data = request.get_json()
    asyncio.create_task(background_process(data))

    return jsonify({"status": "processing"})
```

This sets an important rule of thumb for Flask asynchronous workloads: avoid using them for long-running background tasks. Instead, use a task queue like **RQ** (https://python-rq.org/) or **Celery** (https://docs.celeryq.dev/en/stable/index.html). Consider this rule to guide your design when you have to support several model operations, like multiple database queries, service requests or file operations.

It is also interesting to note that the WsgiToAsgi adapter was developed by the team that supports another of the most popular Python web frameworks in the market: Django, which we will be briefly reviewing at the end of this chapter. In the next section, however, we will review the most Flask-compatible asynchronous-native open-source framework.

Discovering a native asynchronous web framework in Quart

> **Important note**
>
> There are many interesting ASGI frameworks, one of the most popular being FastAPI (`https://fastapi.tiangolo.com/`). As it has already been extensively covered in a number of publications, we have chosen here to focus on Quart because of its simplicity and compatibility with Flask. We do however encourage you to explore other alternatives such as Litestar, Sanic or any of the many open-source projects listed in catalogs like `https://github.com/florimondmanca/awesome-asgi`.

Native asynchronous frameworks like Quart (`https://quart.palletsprojects.com/`) provide full support for the ASGI capabilities implemented by new servers, such as protocols and technologies that extend the scalability of solutions and the scope of alternative approaches to solving complex problems. The applications where asynchronous web frameworks have clear advantages over synchronous or hybrid alternatives include:

- **Implementation of GraphQL servers**: GraphQL is a popular query language (`https://graphql.org/`) to access data models, which defines subscriptions to changes in those data models that can be implemented using long-lived connections.

- **Implementation of the publish–subscribe pattern**: Long-lived connections can be used to push multiple responses to clients that are subscribed simultaneously in a unidirectional way, meaning that several clients receive content pushed by the server simultaneously.

- **Bidirectional real-time data transfers**: By implementing support for the Websocket protocol, ASGI servers can ensure that continuous streams of data are processed from and to the applications.

The concepts listed above are applicable to multiple use cases in which asynchronous programming plays a fundamental role by leveraging non-blocking I/O to access heterogeneous resources. Common examples of such resources include:

- **Conversational user interfaces**: A large language model (LLM) accessible through a chat interface has become one of the dominant forms of artificial intelligence (AI) solution. The generation and delivery of text responses by these models is a good example of an asynchronous use case implementation.

- **Real-time dashboards and monitoring**: One of the most common non-functional requirements in modern software systems is observability, or the ability of a system to support the measurement of its internal status or state.

- **Massive multiplayer games:** The gaming industry uses low-latency, highly concurrent real-time communication among players and game systems, and this is only possible by leveraging continuous data streams handled by asynchronous applications.

- **Internet of Things (IoT) applications**: Vast numbers of sensors are deployed in real-world scenarios to capture information (temperature, light, movement, etc.) that must be persisted, aggregated and processed concurrently.

- **High-concurrency APIs**: Worldwide-scale applications like social media and advertising expose APIs that enable businesses to publish content or digital products, while consumer behavior produces a high number of metrics that must be processed as fast as possible.

As an example, imagine an interviewing system that had to control the time interval for each interview: such a system could not rely on frontend time measurement given that it could be affected by the client's hardware capabilities or be manipulated by users. Instead, you deploy a microservice that provides a continuous stream of reliable date/time instances provided by the public **Network Time Protocol (NTP)** pool of servers. *Figure 7.4* shows the basic schema of the solution:

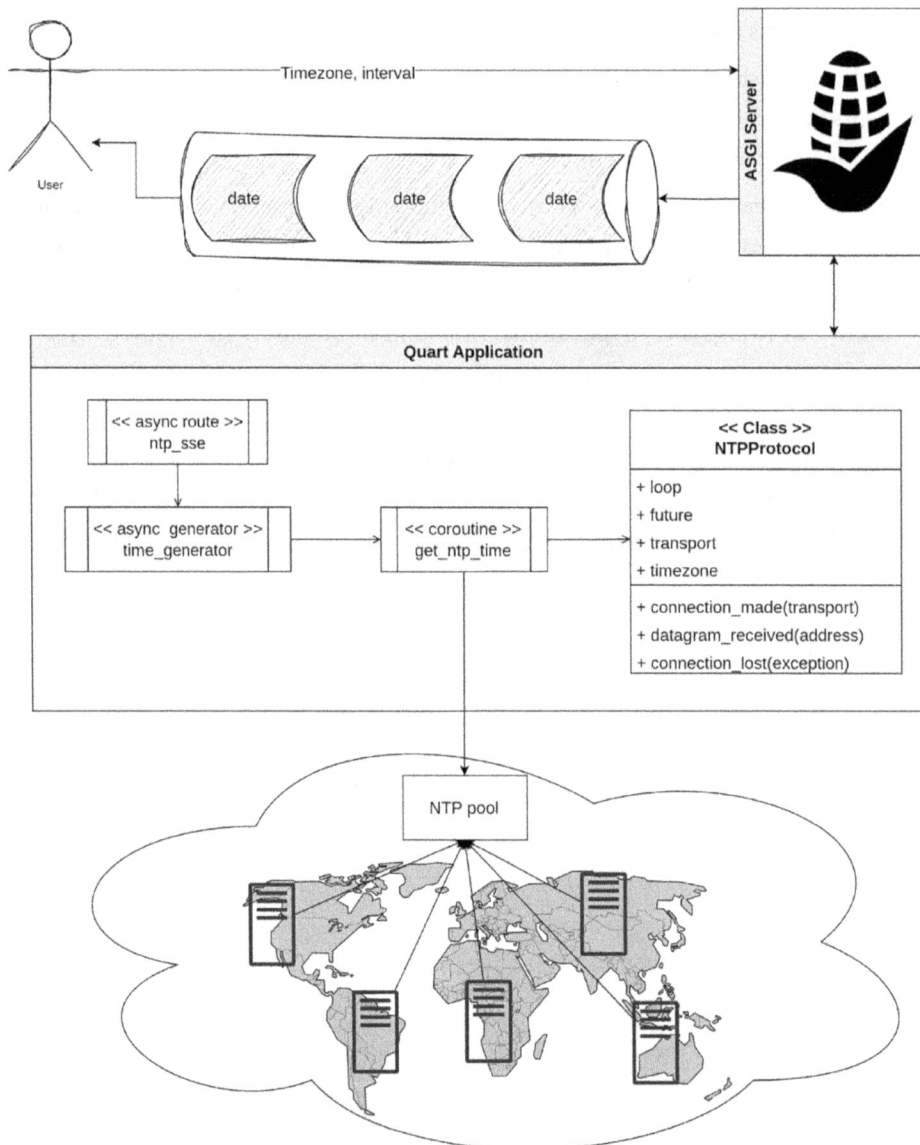

Figure 7.4: MVC server date solution

You might notice that this solution could be deployed near one of the NTP pool servers on any continent, but NTP guarantees you can rely on its accuracy with a higher level of confidence than you can have in the client's clock or even in the clock on your solution-hosting server. We have implemented the use case as a simplified MVC structure. The following code shows an implementation using the Quart framework:

```python
import json
import struct
import asyncio
import datetime
import pytz
from quart import Quart, Response, request


app = Quart(__name__)

class NTPProtocol:
    def __init__(self, loop, timezone):
        self.loop = loop
        self.future = loop.create_future()
        self.transport = None
        self.timezone = timezone

    def connection_made(self, transport):
        self.transport = transport

    def datagram_received(self, data, addr):
        self.future.set_result(data)
        self.transport.close()

    def connection_lost(self, exc):
        if not self.future.done():
            if exc is None:
                self.future.set_exception( Exception("Connection closed"))
            else:
                self.future.set_exception(exc)

async def get_ntp_time(host="pool.ntp.org", timezone="UTC"):
```

```
    port = 123
    address = (host, port)
    msg = b'\x1b' + b'\0' * 47
    TIME1970 = 2208988800
    try:
        loop = asyncio.get_running_loop()
        protocol = NTPProtocol(loop, timezone)
        transport, _ = await loop.create_datagram_endpoint(lambda:
protocol, remote_addr=address)
        transport.sendto(msg)
        data = await protocol.future
        t = struct.unpack("!12I", data)[10]
        t -= TIME1970
        utc_time = datetime.datetime.utcfromtimestamp(t)
        local_tz = pytz.timezone(timezone)
        local_time = utc_time.replace( tzinfo=pytz.utc).astimezone(local_
tz)
        return local_time.strftime("%Y-%m-%d %H:%M:%S %Z%z")
    except Exception as e:
        print(f"Error getting NTP time: {e}")
        return None


async def time_generator(host="pool.ntp.org", timezone="UTC", interval=5):
    while True:
        local_time = await get_ntp_time(host, timezone)
        if local_time:
            yield json.dumps({'time': local_time})
        await asyncio.sleep(interval)


@app.route("/ntp_sse")
async def ntp_sse():
    timezone = request.args.get("timezone", "UTC")
    interval = int(request.args.get("interval", 5))
    async def generate():
        try:
            async for time_data in time_generator(timezone=timezone,
interval=interval):
                yield time_data
```

```
        except pytz.exceptions.UnknownTimeZoneError:
            yield json.dumps({"error": "Invalid timezone"})
        except Exception as e:
            yield json.dumps({"error": e})
    return Response(generate(), mimetype="text/event-stream")


if __name__ == "__main__":
    app.run(debug=True)
```

The model handles the data (the structure required to establish connection with the NTP server) and the logic required to use external service responses (you can access the server when it is running through):

- NTPProtocol class: This class encapsulates the low-level network communication logic for retrieving NTP time. It handles the User Datagram Protocol (UDP) socket connection, data retrieval, and error handling; it represents the data access layer and the core logic for fetching time data.

- get_ntp_time function: This function orchestrates the NTP time retrieval process. It uses NTPProtocol to communicate with the NTP server, performing the necessary data transformations (timestamp to datetime, timezone conversion). This function could also be considered part of the model, since it handles the business logic of time retrieval.

The view in this case is a stream of Server-Sent Events (SSEs) that contain the date transformed from the NTP servers. The time_generator function formats the time data as a JSON-encoded string and the Quart framework itself acts as a view engine that delivers data to the client.

To get user input and orchestrate the solution the /ntp_sse route handler acts as controller. It receives the client's request (including query parameters for time zone and interval), then orchestrates the interaction between the model (get_ntp_time, NTPProtocol) and the view (SSE response). It also handles potential errors (invalid time zone, network issues) and formats error responses.

Notice that in this implementation we have used two low-level functions from the event loop to handle the communication between our solution and the external NTP server. In the NTPProtocol class, an asyncio.Future object is used to represent the eventual result of the asynchronous operation (receiving the NTP data), and in this way we can continue to execute other tasks while waiting for the network operation to complete.

The get_ntp_time function uses the event loop create_datagram_endpoint() function to establish a non-blocking UDP socket connection, and then by using the datagram_received() and connection_lost() methods from the NTPProtocol class instance it resolves the asyncio.Future (https://docs.python.org/3/library/asyncio-future.html), signaling the completion of the network operation.

Quart and other minimalist native-asynchronous web frameworks can be also used in serverless computing scenarios, where there may be restrictions on compute or resource availability. This kind of deployment scenario is usually suitable for data transformation rather than data transference.

Other web frameworks, such as Django, also support asynchronous capabilities, but given their more feature-rich dev experience (including access to an object-relational mapper, native support for authentication and data model administration, among other goodies), you must validate the support for asynchronous programming in those features and extensions before deploying them in ASGI environments, especially third party apps, plugins and middleware.

Reviewing Django asynchronous support

The long journey to support for asynchronous programming in Django started in version 3.0, released at the end of 2019. The first approach was the previously mentioned asgiref adapter, which allowed WSGI applications to be deployed in ASGI servers. This is one of the most important modules because it brings the sync_to_async (https://docs.djangoproject.com/en/5.1/topics/async/#asgiref.sync.sync_to_async) function/decorator, which lets you wrap a synchronous piece of code into an asynchronous function that can be run in the same main execution thread as the main request or in a separate thread context.

There have been many other improvements to the Django ecosystem's asynchronous support, the following diagram showing a timeline of the principal asynchronous features released per version:

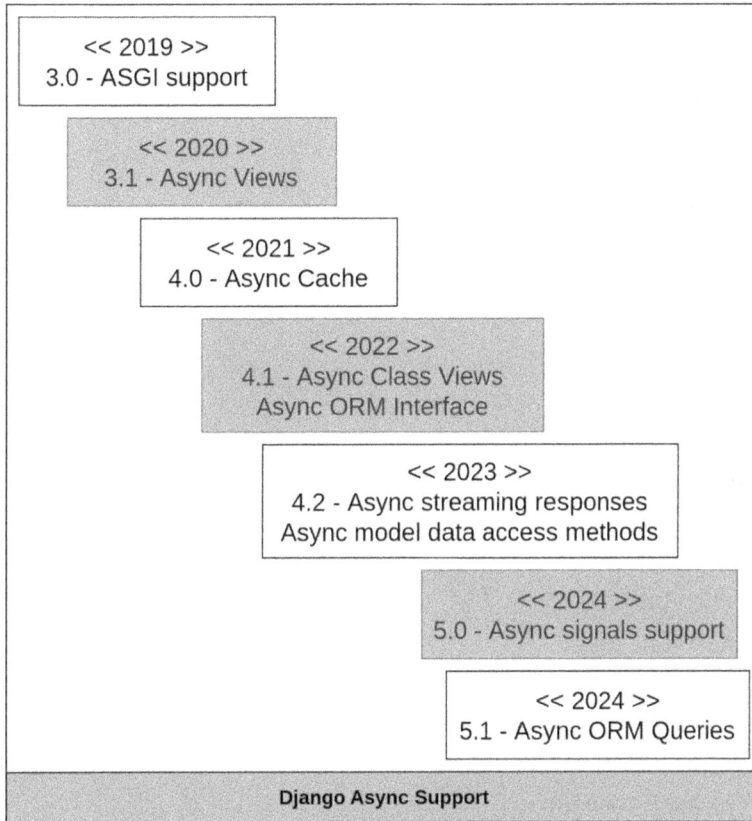

Figure 7.5: Django async support evolution

The basic concepts we have described for Flask apply to Django, so if for example you deploy your application behind a WSGI server your code will run synchronously even if it is intended to be asynchronous (`async/await`). In addition, extensions/middleware for both frameworks must also be asynchronous-compatible, or else processing of the entire request will be handled in a synchronous way; this is especially important in the Django ecosystem given the long list of middleware available for the framework.

Currently, Django async views can be extended with a wide range of decorators. This mechanism includes support for caching, compression, security or even access methods. You can consult Django-specific documentation to check the capabilities of each individual decorator in what is quite a long list:

- `cache_control()`
- `condition()`
- `conditional_page()`
- `csrf_exempt()`
- `csrf_protect()`
- `ensure_csrf_cookie()`
- `etag()`
- `gzip_page()`
- `last_modified()`
- `never_cache()`
- `no_append_slash()`
- `require_GET()`
- `require_http_methods()`
- `require_POST()`
- `require_safe()`
- `requires_csrf_token()`
- `sensitive_post_parameters()`
- `sensitive_variables()`
- `vary_on_cookie()`
- `vary_on_headers()`
- `xframe_options_deny()`
- `xframe_options_exempt()`
- `xframe_options_sameorigin()`

The **Object-Relational Mapping (ORM)** pattern/anti-pattern is deeply supported in Django to access data stores (usually relational databases). Asynchronous ORM support started in version 4.1 of Django and will be one of the topics of our next chapter.

Summary

Web frameworks constitute one of the most widely used tools in the Python ecosystem. The breadth of their solution space has proven its usefulness across a range of use cases, starting with classical CRUD applications and taking in data pipelines, REST and GraphQL APIs, and intensive UI experiences. Asynchronous programming extends their capabilities to new horizons of scalability by providing support for new protocols and technologies.

In this chapter we have instrumented two of the most popular hybrid Python synchronous/asynchronous frameworks: Flask and Django. That instrumentation requires not only changes to support asynchronous code but also changes to the way in which it is executed.

Both frameworks evolved to derive some of the benefits of the asynchronous paradigm without disrupting the developer experience or deployment requirements. Nevertheless, new frameworks offering native support provide clear benefits for clean-sheet projects by leveraging the capabilities of asynchronous web servers or serverless execution environments.

In the next chapter we are going to concentrate our attention on another of the major use cases in which asynchronous programming can benefit your solutions: data access. Data is the lifeblood of many systems, and applying asynchronous programming to interactions with data stores provides important advantages in modern environments.

8

Asynchronous Data Access

Data is the lifeblood of a system. In many applications, you start with data that is noisy and inconsistent, and you try to structure and regularize it by applying a variety of data-wrangling methods. In recent years there has been a revolution in our understanding of data and the techniques available for processing it, mostly fueled by the volume of data available. The number of datapoints captured by sensors, actuators, devices and systems makes a case for what is known as data-driven decision-making. When it comes to supporting those decisions, traditional synchronous data-access methods often fall short, because of expectations for short response times – you have to give answers on short timescales but are often working with way more data than before.

In this scenario asynchronous programming can be a valuable tool to scale up the amount of data a system can process, providing a definite advantage in some situations. Our explorations will center on structured data access techniques, but will also touch on other data engineering tasks. This subject is vast and we encourage you to dig deeper to get a sense of the full potential and implications of asynchronous data tasks.

In this chapter we'll be covering:

- Understanding Python's API for database connectors
- Making use of in-process databases
- Accessing external databases
- Using object-relational mappers

Technical requirements

In this chapter we will use a number of external packages in addition to the standard Python library to explore database engines, including database connection drivers and a simple object-relational mapper. As usual the source code is available in the relevant chapter folder of the Github repo (`https://github.com/PacktPublishing/Asynchronous-Programming-in-Python`).

In addition, to run the code for the external database examples you will need to install **PostgreSQL** (`https://www.postgresql.org/download/`) or use a container like Docker (`https://www.docker.com/blog/how-to-use-the-postgres-docker-official-image/`) or Podman (`https://podman-desktop.io/tutorial/interacting-with-a-database-server`) that runs PostgreSQL and gives you access to it using port 5432. Remember to generate a virtual environment exclusively for the chapter, so that the additional packages do not interfere with other requirements:

```
$ python3 -m venv .env
$ pip install -r requirements.txt
$ docker run --rm --name postgres-db -p 5432:5432 -e POSTGRES_
PASSWORD=postgres -d postgres
```

The last command uses docker to run a local postgresql server accessible through port 5432 with the username *postgres* and password *postgres*.

Understanding Python's API for database connectors

Structured data has been the principal paradigm for data management for the last 50 years, and the foundations of data modeling, persistence and information retrieval are usually viewed through the lens of the **relational data model** (proposed by Edgar Codd in the 1970s – `https://www.seas.upenn.edu/~zives/03f/cis550/codd.pdf`).

In the last few decades non-relational databases have also gained traction for specific use cases: *document-oriented databases* to represent schemaless or dynamically schemed data, *key-value databases* used as cache storage, *graph databases* to store highly related data, *timeseries databases* to store and query datapoints collected by sensors, etc.

No matter what type of data store you use, the basic data operations that can be performed over a set of data points can be assigned to four categories:

- **Access**: Every time you consume an entire data collection from a source, or you filter a subset from a data source, you are reading data. The source can be files, databases, streams or some other systematic representation. This kind of operation is usually the most asynchronous-friendly, inasmuch as many consumers can make use of the data source without disturbing each other.

- **Mutation**: Data can be generated/updated/deleted from multiple inputs like signals, deliberated actions, or events. The modifications made into the persistence mechanism are mutations; for example if nothing was previously recorded and data is then persisted for the first time, it is created, and thus the mechanism was mutated from nothing to something. In a similar way, alterations to the data persisted are also mutations. These kinds of operation are the most problematic from the asynchronous point of view, given that simultaneous mutations have the potential to create data consistency issues. Relational database engines guarantee reliability and consistency in database transactions by providing support for the **ACID model**, the acronym standing for Atomicity, Consistency, Isolation, and Durability:

    - *Atomicity*: A database transaction is a set of actions that cannot be divided, which means that you can trust that all the actions in the set were executed completely, never partially.

    - *Consistency*: Each database transaction is guaranteed to change the database from one valid state to another valid state from a data integrity point of view; it means that a transaction always follows any specified data validation rules.

    - *Isolation*: Concurrent transactions over a relational database have the same effect as if they were executed in a sequence.

    - *Durability*: Transactions affect the database permanently, meaning that changes are persistent over engine crashes, restarts or anomaly events.

    Postgresql supports various levels of ACID compliance; for more information please refer to the excellent documentation on transactions and concurrency at database level available at https://www.postgresql.org/docs/current/mvcc.html.

    Other database engines apply similar concepts in different contexts, for example non-relational databases apply the BASE paradigm (Basically Available, Soft state, Eventually consistent).

- **Arrangement**: Sorting and ordering operations are transformations applied to the data once it is read from the origin, but such changes might not be persistent. Hence although they are alterations of the data, they are usually not associated with the mutation of data itself. These kinds of operation are asynchronous-friendly because they are often performed in random access memory spaces.

- **Consolidation**: Another type of operation is the generation of new data based on previous data, for example analytical aggregations of quantitative measures from raw data. Take for example the calculation of the disk space consumed by several files: the result is metadata generated from existing data. Consolidations and aggregations are core to business intelligence use cases.

Python has standardized the way that providers and communities should implement access to a data store by defining, in PEP 249 (Python Database API Specification v2.0, `https://peps.python.org/pep-0249/`), the basic constructs that any database driver is expected to include. The two main concepts are **Connection** and **Cursor**.

Cursors provide context for database operations, opened by `Connection` instances which are established to the database server. Cursors opened from a single connection are not isolated, which means that mutations made by a cursor are instantly available for other cursors opened in the same connection, but might not be visible to cursors opened in different connections – it depends on the configuration of isolation levels that the connection uses with the database server.

Python's DB API 2.0 is implemented by several database drivers for **in-process databases** (database servers that run in the same process as Python) and external servers (which require the transfer of data between Python processes and the database server). Initially it handled each operation synchronously but more recently has included support for asynchronous implementations.

Making use of in-process databases

In-process databases provide the full database server experience running *inside* the same process as Python execution, which means you have access to the full capabilities of the database engine but without the network latency, authentication and authorization, or protocol change trade-offs. *Figure 8.1* shows the basic scheme for this type of deployment:

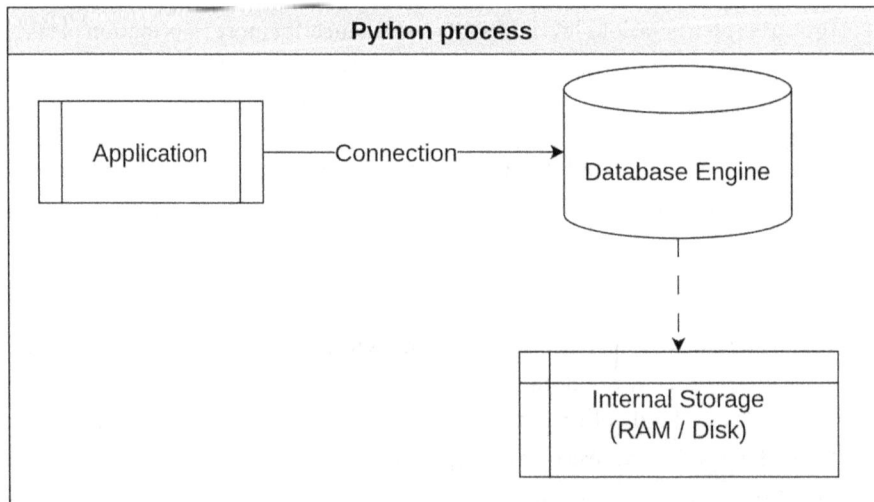

Figure 8.1: In-process database engines

Running a database server this way doesn't limit the capabilities of the database engine, and there's a wide range of in-process databases that provide the same features as their external-server counterparts. Several popular in-process databases are available commercially, while the following list shows some of the open-source alternatives for various use cases:

- **Sqlite:** The most popular Python embedded database (`https://sqlite.org/mostdeployed.html`). It is an OnLine Transactional Processing (OLTP) system, which means you can use it to deploy structures that follow the relational model. Usually the data modeled is balanced between access and mutation workloads, taking advantage of the normal forms (`https://en.wikipedia.org/wiki/Database_normalization`).

- **Duckdb:** An interesting approach that has taken off recently is to use an in-process database for OnLine Analytical Processing (OLAP). This alternative provides a rich subset of standard **SQL (Structured Query Language)** focused on access, arrangement and consolidating workloads in datasets that might exceed the total available RAM (`https://duckdb.org/why_duckdb#fast`).

- **TinyDB:** Document-oriented databases are part of the **NoSQL** (Not Only SQL) family which has become popular over recent decades, providing an alternative for storing semi-structured data using the ubiquitous **JavaScript Object Notation (JSON)**. TinyDB is a Python-native implementation (`https://tinydb.readthedocs.io/en/latest/intro.html#why-use-tinydb`) that is not SQL-compliant but which provides basic support for access/mutation/arrangement/consolidation operations through a well-known API.

- **Kuzu:** A graph database built to analyze large networks (`https://github.com/kuzudb/kuzu`), this is an interesting option for modeling data using nodes and links. The Cypher query language is rather different from SQL but analogous in some respects. Graph databases received a boost in popularity in the market following the introduction of the knowledge graph concept by a number of prominent companies.

- **LanceDB:** More recently the artificial Intelligence wave has brought attention to new mechanisms for managing and querying data, in this case **vector databases** like **LanceDB** (`https://lancedb.github.io/lancedb/`) and Chroma (`https://docs.trychroma.com`). These store and query vector representations of raw data (the vectors are called embeddings) which are usually produced by a pre-trained machine learning model and then used to perform similarity search.

There are many other purpose-specific in-process databases, and one of the key characteristics you must always dig into is how the engine manages concurrency. The engine's concurrency management policy sets limits on the asynchronous data access gains the engine can provide:

- **Blocking engines**: Their access model blocks concurrent access when applying some operations, usually mutations, and this might impose a strong restriction for some write-intensive use cases. An example of this kind of engine is Sqlite (`https://sqlite.org/draft/wal.html`).

- **Thread-level control**: In this model, concurrent operations can be initiated from multiple threads. However, in Python the global interpreter lock (GIL) means that only one Python thread can actively execute Python bytecode at a time. While underlying database engines (often written in C/C++ like DuckDB) can release the GIL during heavy computational work, allowing internal parallelism, frequent GIL re-acquisition or Python-bound database interactions can still serialize Python threads, potentially blocking others. An example of this type of engine is DuckDB (`https://duckdb.org/docs/stable/connect/concurrency#concurrency-within-a-single-process`).

- **Fully asynchronous**: The most recent engines include fully non-blocking I/O operations, which means you can take full advantage of the asynchronous programming features we have already discussed. In this kind of engine, mutations include not only direct data operations like create, update or delete but also versioning, schema evolution and data indexing. A good example is LanceDB.

As an example we are going to load 1000 fine food reviews from a public dataset (`https://cookbook.openai.com/examples/get_embeddings_from_dataset`) with pre-calculated embeddings into a `Sqlite` database using the most (currently) popular asynchronous interface library:

```python
import asyncio
import csv
import sqlite3
import aiosqlite


async def create_table(db_path, table_name, column_names):
    async with aiosqlite.connect(db_path) as db:
        columns_str = ", ".join(f"{col} TEXT" for col in column_names)
        create_table_sql = f"CREATE TABLE IF NOT EXISTS {table_name} ({columns_str})"
        await db.execute(create_table_sql)
        await db.commit()
```

```python
            print(f"Table '{table_name}' created (or already existed).")

async def insert_data(db_path, table_name, data):
    try:
        async with aiosqlite.connect(db_path) as db:
            columns = ", ".join(data.keys())
            placeholders = ", ".join("?" * len(data))
            values = tuple(data.values())
            insert_sql = f"INSERT INTO {table_name} ({columns}) VALUES
({placeholders})"
            await db.execute(insert_sql, values)
            await db.commit()
    except sqlite3.OperationalError as e:
        if "database is locked" in str(e):
            print("Database is locked for writing...")
        else:
            raise e

async def process_csv_and_insert(db_path, table_name, csv_file_path):
    data_list = []
    column_names = []
    with open(csv_file_path, 'r', encoding='utf-8') as csvfile:
        reader = csv.DictReader(csvfile)
        column_names = reader.fieldnames
        for row in reader:
            data_list.append(row)

    await create_table(db_path, table_name, column_names)
    tasks = [insert_data(db_path, table_name, data) for data in data_list]
    await asyncio.gather(*tasks)

async def main():
    db_path = "async.sqlite"
    table_name = "async_filled"
    csv_file_path = "fine_food_reviews_with_embeddings_1k.csv"
    await process_csv_and_insert(db_path, table_name, csv_file_path)

if __name__ == "__main__":
    asyncio.run(main())
```

- The code uses three asynchronous functions to create the data structure, load the original CSV file into a list, and then concurrently try to insert the data into the database. It's a simple simulation of multiple clients trying to operate over a single data structure which they have persisted to disk.

- Although trivial, the previous example shows a common hard limit for asynchronous data access in Python. The main restriction you often encounter is not the client-side access mode (synchronous/asynchronous) but the actual database engine concurrency management policy. When you run the example, you will notice that there are several write-blocks:

```
$ python sqlite_async.py
Table 'async_filled' created (or already existed).
Database is locked for writing...
Database is locked for writing...
```

The same example implemented using an asynchronous native database engine like LanceDB shows a similar issue:

```
$ python lancedb_async.py
[2025-04-15T23:21:31Z WARN lance::dataset::write::insert] No existing
dataset at tmp/async_lancedb/async_filled.lance, it will be created
Table 'async_filled' created (or already existed).
Error writing into database...lance error: Commit conflict for version
923: Failed to commit the transaction after 20 retries., /root/.cargo/
registry/src/index.crates.io-6f17d22bba15001f/lance-0.25.0/src/io/commit.
rs:880:19
Error writing into database...lance error: Commit conflict for version
927: Failed to commit the transaction after 20 retries., /root/.cargo/
registry/src/index.crates.io-6f17d22bba15001f/lance-0.25.0/src/io/commit.
rs:880:19
```

In both cases we hit a wall, and in the end it doesn't matter whether the engine driver is an asynchronous interface to the engine or a native client; you have to handle the possible concurrency errors in an explicit way.

Important note

In-process database engines are some of the most interesting and useful resources in the current data landscape. There are several software patterns that can be used to handle situations like the one the example presented, including circuit-breaker, multi-version concurrency control, or two-phase locking. We encourage you to explore those patterns based on your specific use case.

Accessing external databases

The predominant architecture for storing an application's data and state is the client/server model. In this model, a database engine server/cluster handles all the data storage, connectivity and query capabilities, and multiple clients use a protocol to communicate with the server and wait for the results of their operations. Database servers usually have several techniques for minimizing wait times, but with large datasets or with untuned queries the waiting or data transfer times can be long. This is a perfect scenario in which to develop database drivers (connectors) that optimize the client's resources by not blocking the execution process/thread/coroutine over those time windows. *Figure 8.2* illustrates this model:

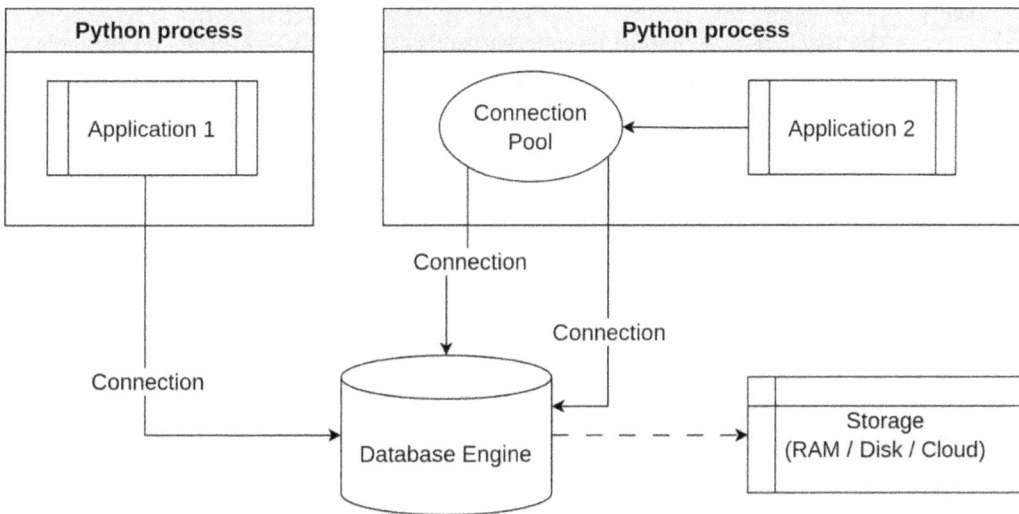

Figure 8.2: Client/Server database engines

The diagram shows two types of application, one that directly opens connections to the database engine, just as in the previous section where we worked directly with the engine in the same processes, while the second application uses a mechanism called a **connection pool**, which is a buffer of open connections to the database that can be reused on multiple occasions. The idea is that given the high relative cost of starting a new connection to the database server, a client opens multiple connections and keeps them open even if they are not being used all the time. When a database operation is required, one of the pool connections can be used instead of a new one.

As with in-process databases you can find many general and purpose-specific databases that follow this client/server architecture. We will focus now on using what has been described by its proponents as the '*The World's Most Advanced Open Source Relational Database*' (https://www.postgresql.org/), and will do so in an asynchronous way to illustrate the benefits of connection pooling. The following piece of code compares the time required to complete several operations that open direct connections versus using a pool provided by the client:

> **Important note**
>
> The following piece of code includes *hardcoded* parameters for accessing the database engine. This approach is only useful for demonstration purposes and should never be used in testing/production code. Please check the many security guides available online to improve the code properly.

```python
import time
import asyncio
import asyncpg
host="127.0.0.1"
user="postgres"
password="postgres"

async def bench_asyncpg_con():
    power = 2
    start = time.monotonic()
    for i in range(1, 1000):
        con = await asyncpg.connect(user=user, password=password,
host=host)
        await con.fetchval('select 2 ^ $1', power)
        await con.close()
    end = time.monotonic()
    print(end - start, "Seconds for direct connection version")

async def bench_asyncpg_pool():
    pool = await asyncpg.create_pool(user=user, password=password,
host=host)
    power = 2
    start = time.monotonic()
```

```
    for i in range(1, 1000):
        async with pool.acquire() as con:
            await con.fetchval('select 2 ^ $1', power)
    await pool.close()
    end = time.monotonic()
    print(end - start, "Seconds for pool version")

async def main():
    await bench_asyncpg_con()
    await bench_asyncpg_pool()

if name == "main":
    asyncio.run(main())
```

In this case we have used **asyncpg** (`https://magicstack.github.io/asyncpg/current/`) as our driver; alternatives you might like to check out include *psycopg3* (`https://www.psycopg.org/psycopg3/docs/index.html`) and *aiopg* (`https://aiopg.readthedocs.io/en/stable/index.html`).

Asyncpg is a native asynchronous implementation of the PostgreSQL communication protocol, it has the largest community of the three options, and in some benchmarks is faster than the alternatives (`https://gistpreview.github.io/?0ed296e93523831ea0918d42dd1258c2`). Psycopg3 provides a sync and an async Python interface so is suitable for the two types of workloads, its community is active and the documentation is very helpful. Aiopg is a thin asynchronous wrapper over the well-established synchronous driver Psycopg2.

To run the test you must start your local PostgreSQL engine before running the code or the container image. For our test we are going to use the official PostgreSQL Docker image, mapping the local port 5432 to allow access from the code:

```
$ docker run --name localpg -p 5432:5432 -e POSTGRES_PASSWORD=postgres -d
postgres
```

Then, in another terminal session, when you run the sample code you can see the difference between the two connection methods:

```
$ python pg_connection_pool.py
33.563900804001605 Seconds for direct connection version
0.2807244890136644 Seconds for pool version
```

The connection pool is also configurable with respect to parameters such as minimum/maximum number of open connections, connection timeout, and maximum number of queries executed before a connection is closed and replaced by a new one. These settings might have an impact on the memory consumption of your applications and/or their overall performance.

Retrieving data efficiently

One of the most interesting applications of the Python Database API Specification 2.0 (PEP-249) is the concept of a Cursor, which is like a session over a connection to the database. Queries are used to execute operations that might return large amounts of data (access operations), and normally such read queries would return all the results and load them into memory. However, this might be less efficient than using pagination techniques or, even better, using the power of Python generators to continuously return data until all the results are returned. The following example shows a simple comparison of the three techniques:

```python
import asyncio
import asyncpg


host="127.0.0.1"
user="postgres"
password="postgres"


async def create_connection pool():
    pool = await asyncpg.create_pool(user=user, password=password,
host=host)
    return pool


async def generate_rows(pool, table_name):
    async with pool.acquire() as conn:
        await conn.execute(f"""
CREATE TABLE IF NOT EXISTS {table_name} (id SERIAL PRIMARY KEY,name
TEXT,value INTEGER)""")
        await conn.execute(f"TRUNCATE TABLE {table_name}")
        await conn.executemany(
            f"INSERT INTO {table_name} (name, value) VALUES ($1, $2)",
            [(f"row {i}", i) for i in range(1,100000)]
        )


async def fetch_all_in_memory(pool, table_name):
```

```
        try:
            async with pool.acquire() as conn:
                query = f"SELECT * FROM {table_name}"
                rows = await conn.fetch(query)
                print(f"Fetched {len(rows)} rows into memory.")
                return [tuple(row) for row in rows]
        except Exception as e:
            print(f"Error fetching all data in memory: {e}")
            return []


async def fetch_in_pages(pool, table_name, page_size = 10000):
    all_rows = []
    offset = 0
    try:
        async with pool.acquire() as conn:
            async with conn.transaction():
                cursor = await conn.cursor(f"SELECT * FROM {table_name}")
                while True:
                    rows = await cursor.fetch(page_size)
                    if len(rows) < 1:
                        break
                    all_rows.extend([tuple(row) for row in rows])
                    print(f"Fetched page {(offset/page_size)+1}")
                    offset += page_size
        print(f"Fetched {len(all_rows)} rows using pagination.")
        return all_rows
    except Exception as e:
        print(f"Error fetching data with pagination: {e}")
        return []


async def fetch_as_generator(pool, table_name):
    try:
        async with pool.acquire() as conn:
            async with conn.transaction():
                query = f"SELECT * FROM {table_name}"
                async for row in conn.cursor(query):
                    yield tuple(row)
        print(f"Generator created for fetching rows from {table_name}")
    except Exception as e:
```

```
        print(f"Error creating generator: {e}")
        yield None

async def main():
    pool = await create_connection_pool()
    table_name = "sample_table"
    await generate_rows(pool, table_name)
    all_rows = await fetch_all_in_memory(pool, table_name)
    paged_rows = await fetch_in_pages(pool, table_name)
    total_rows = 0
    async for row in fetch_as_generator(pool, table_name):
        total_rows += 1
    print(f"Rows fetched from generator: {total_rows}")
    await pool.close()

if __name__ == "__main__":
    asyncio.run(main())
```

The fetch_all_in_memory function might be the fastest for a small number of rows, but its memory consumption increases proportionately with the number of records returned. Paged fetch_in_pages retrieval improves the situation by consuming less memory, but requires several round trips to the database, which might be less efficient. Finally, the generator function fetch_as_generator can be useful for handling data streaming use cases.

As we have seen, the gains from asynchronous programming for database access depend on the specific use case and the capabilities of the engine. The take-away is that it's important to understand how your engine handles concurrency for access/mutation operations and the context in which you'll be accessing your data.

Using object-relational mappers

An **object-relational mapper (ORM)** is a piece of software that tries to handle the 'impedance mismatch' between the relational database model and the object-oriented paradigm (https://en.wikipedia.org/wiki/Object%E2%80%93relational_impedance_mismatch). Since its first iterations ORMs have been the center of heated debates, Martin Fowler some time ago writing a great piece on the general landscape that is still valuable today (https://martinfowler.com/bliki/OrmHate.html). In the Python world the use of ORMs is common; *Figure 8.3* summarizes their capabilities:

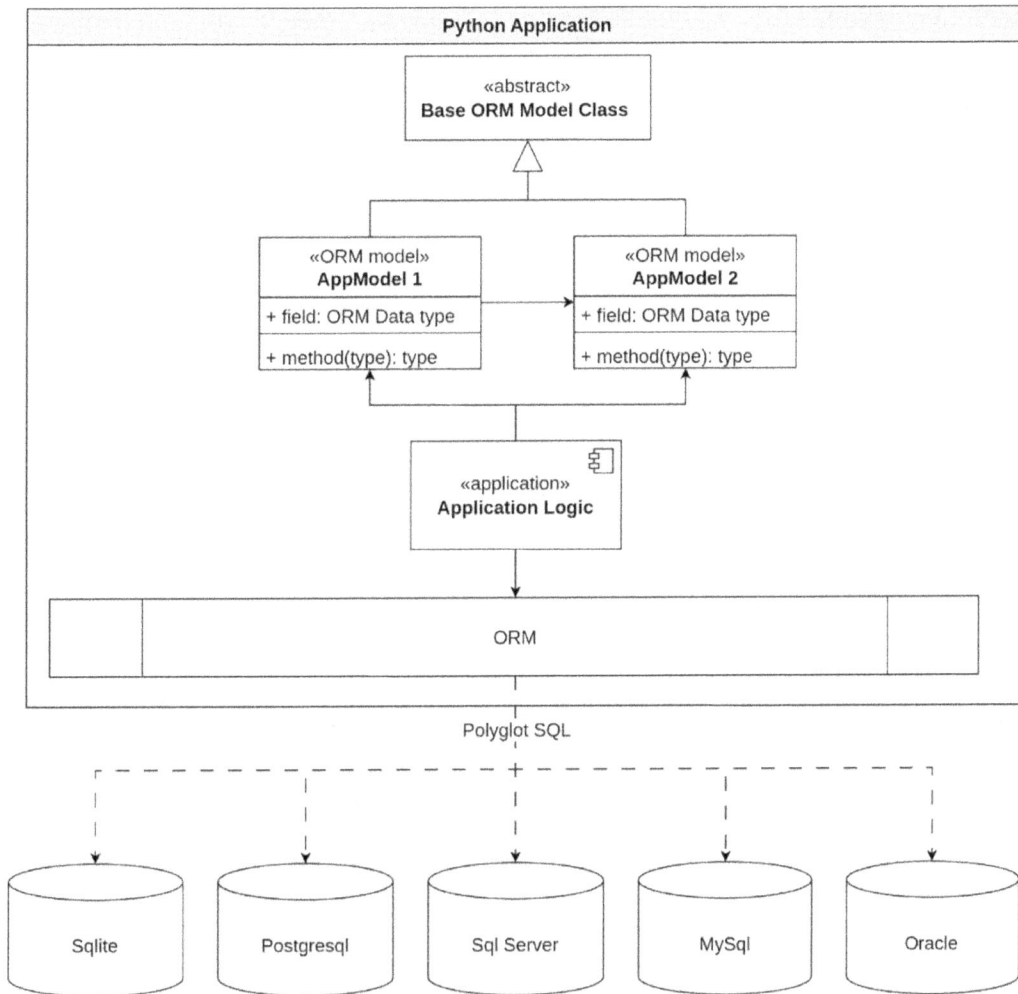

Figure 8.3: ORM general model

We are not going to argue the pros and cons of ORMs in depth, but notice that there are, as with many other projects in the ecosystem, several implementations that provide differing levels of asynchronous support. The main advantages provided by ORMs include:

- Reduction of SQL code, allowing development with unified Python code
- Standardized and secure data-access techniques
- Centralized schema and relationship definitions in data models
- Schema change handling through version-controlled migrations
- Polyglot database engine access

But as you might already know, *there is no such thing as a free lunch* (https://en.wikipedia.org/wiki/No_such_thing_as_a_free_lunch), and ORMs have been associated with a variety of architectural concerns, performance penalties and in some cases bad practices. Criteria useful for checking whether an ORM is suitable for your use case include:

- Simple/CRUD-heavy: If your application primarily involves basic Create, Read, Update, and Delete (CRUD) operations on well-defined relational models then an ORM is usually an excellent fit. It significantly reduces boilerplate SQL, makes code more readable, and speeds up development.

- Complex/performance-critical queries: If your use case frequently requires highly optimized, complex SQL queries (e.g. deeply nested joins, analytical queries, custom aggregations, stored procedures, or very large data sets where raw SQL performance is paramount), an ORM can sometimes be a hindrance. While most ORMs offer ways to drop down to raw SQL when needed, forcing them to generate extremely complex queries can lead to inefficient SQL or make the ORM code overly convoluted.

- ORM responsibilities: Which responsibilities delegate on your ORM? ORMs create classes that transact with the database, represent records of a table, and manage relationships between the data model. Some ORMs even create and execute migrations of DDL (Data Definition Language) and DML (Data Manipulation Language) SQL statements.

As an example of how to use a simple-yet-asynchronous ORM tool (TortoiseORM – https://tortoise.github.io/index.html), we are going to use two related models (an Author who writes several Books) to illustrate the asynchronous operations that an ORM abstracts:

```python
import asyncio
from tortoise import Tortoise, run_async, fields
from tortoise.models import Model

class Author(Model):
    id = fields.IntField(pk=True)
    name = fields.CharField(max_length=255)
    books: fields.ReverseRelation["Book"]
    def __str__(self):
        return self.name
    class Meta:
        ordering = ["name"]

class Book(Model):
```

```
    id = fields.IntField(pk=True)
    title = fields.CharField(max_length=255)
    author: fields.ForeignKeyRelation[Author] = fields.
ForeignKeyField("models.Author", related_name="books")
    publication_date = fields.DateField(null=True)

    def __str__(self):
        return self.title
    class Meta:
        ordering = ["title"]

async def main():
    await Tortoise.init(db_url="sqlite://:memory:", modules={"models":
["__main__"]},)
    await Tortoise.generate_schemas()
    print("--- Creating Authors ---")
    ...


if __name__ == "__main__":
    run_async(main())
```

Notice that no SQL code is involved in this example, and there is no pool of connections to be handled. The fact that we have delegated several data management tasks to the ORM might have an impact in the long term – for example, the models (Author and Book) are tightly coupled to the ORM implementation and inherit the data mapping and access methods from the base Model class defined by the ORM. Tight dependency on external frameworks is one of the classic *code smells* in Clean Architecture theory (https://blog.cleancoder.com/uncle-bob/2012/08/13/the-clean-architecture.html).

There are also abstractions built over ORMs that can speed up build times for Python solutions, for example SQL Model (https://sqlmodel.tiangolo.com/) which is built over Pydantic (https://docs.pydantic.dev/latest/), and SQLAlchemy (https://sqlalchemy.org/). SQL Model simplifies interacting with SQL databases for the popular FastAPI framework, but as with any other tool, it is beneficial to understand the trade-offs involved in its use in the short and long term.

While the immediate benefits of ORMs in reducing boilerplate and simplifying initial development are evident, this convenience often comes at the cost of reduced control and the introduction of potential performance bottlenecks. ORMs abstract away the complexities of SQL query optimization, and that can lead to inefficient queries for complex data retrieval or large-scale operations. Developers relying heavily on ORMs might lose proficiency in writing efficient raw SQL, making it harder to diagnose and fix performance issues when they arise. Furthermore, the impedance mismatch between object-oriented programming paradigms and relational database structures can sometimes force developers into awkward modeling choices or require verbose ORM configurations to achieve the desired database schema, potentially complicating schema evolution or specific database features.

Summary

In this chapter we have explored three ways to operate over data using asynchronous programming. In many use cases, the management of state in an application requires the inclusion of a database server to persist the data, which is a good fit for asynchronous programming. In Python there are several ways to harness database engines:

- As in-process tools that handle direct connections from your source code
- As external dependencies in a client/server architecture
- As an abstraction provided by ORMs

Finally, remember that databases are not the only way to handle structured data in Python, and that other use cases exist that involve data wrangling and which could benefit from asynchronous programming. In the following chapter we're going to explore one of the most important of these: data pipelines.

9

Asynchronous Data Pipelines

From the early 2010s onwards, multiple companies rushed into developing frameworks and tools to handle the 'Big Data' they generated, but many discovered that the amount of data processed was in fact rather small. The problem was that traditional techniques were often found wanting when it came to processing the data available in new formats and structures.

There were business lessons there, but the response from the tech industry was to flex the boundaries of traditional processing models and offer lightweight, local-first solutions for processing data. A well-written sequence of independent but related data processing tasks is the common basis from which technology and product teams start when designing processes today.

A common use case is the processing of datasets, where a dataset is a collection of related data. In a perfect world all data would be well structured and consistent, but in real-life situations you typically need to perform a variety of tasks on your data as a series of repeatable steps to make it suitable for business applications.

In this chapter you will learn how to leverage the power of asynchronous programming to design data pipelines that work with datasets in an efficient way. We'll be covering the following main topics:

- Understanding data pipelines
- Working with data pipelines
- Scaling data pipelines for cloud environments

Technical requirements

We will be looking at two different implementations of a common data pipeline example. You can find the code in the Chapter09 folder of the Github repo (https://github.com/PacktPublishing/Asynchronous-Programming-in-Python). It is recommended that you create a new virtual environment inside the folder and then run each Python file to check its output. No external packages are required, but this way you can isolate your execution from the common Python environment of your computer:

```
$ python3 -m venv .env
```

Understanding data pipelines

A **data pipeline** is a mechanism to handle three types of operation over data: extraction, transformation, and load. *Extraction* is the process of obtaining raw data from a source, i.e. data that hasn't been processed previously. Imagine extracting images from a camera, recordings from sensors in the wild, or text from comments on a website.

The *transformation* process takes data points and applies functions to clean (filter), enrich, validate, change or project the original raw data in order to make it processable in business applications. The transformations can be handled sequentially or in parallel, and might involve long and complex computational operations or small incremental steps. Most importantly, transformations must handle edge cases and exceptions in a consistent manner, because raw data is usually messy.

Load operations, the third type of operation common in data pipelines, involve a series of steps to connect and store data to be persisted in some way. Traditionally, these operations would load transformed data into a relational database, but modern cloud technologies like object storage services and computation-storage decoupling have changed this idea radically.

While data pipelines have traditionally performed operations in the order extraction – transform – load (ETL), computer science research, supported by cloud computing possibilities, has given rise to new capabilities, such as processing transformations inside of data stores in extraction – load – transform (ELT) order. The difference is not trivial: the decision as to which approach to adopt can have implications for availability, resilience, and other architectural aspects of an implementation. The following diagram illustrates the two approaches:

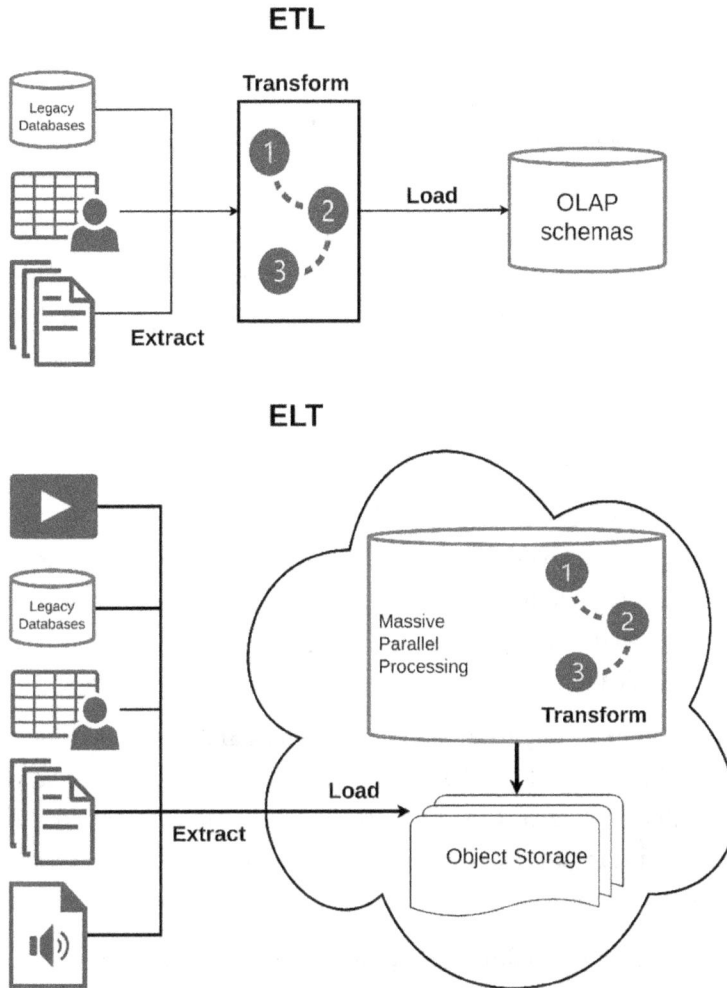

Figure 9.1: ETL vs. ELT processes

Notice that traditional ETL data pipelines rely on three types of container (using the C4 Model definition of container available at https://c4model.com/abstractions/container): *data source* (usually structured data), *transformation server/application*, and *destination data store* (usually another structured system).

ELT, on the other hand, relies on the ability of the destination data store to perform transformations. This is a key distinction, with responsibility for both the loading and transforming steps implying that data processing and storage are mixed within the same container (again, using the C4 Model concept of container). This means that network latencies, access control and security aspects are concentrated in a single unit of processing.

Cloud-native data warehouses are particularly well-suited for ELT because they decouple processing from storage, allowing each to be scaled independently based on the workload but maintaining the consistency of a single container. For example, when ingesting (loading) data, the system needs to scale storage capacity, while processing needs may remain constant. Conversely, during transformation tasks a significant increase in processing power is needed, while storage may only require a moderate increase. This architectural flexibility is a major advantage of the ELT model.

The Pipes and Filters architecture

In previous chapters we have explored techniques that can be used to design extraction and load systems, while in this section we are going to concentrate on a simple pipeline execution system, seeing it as an abstraction to help understand where asynchronous programming makes sense for transformation workloads.

A data pipeline executor is an implementation of the **Pipes and Filters architectural pattern**, in which each step is known as a filter. Each step must be self-contained and be able to receive messages from an inbound pipe. It then applies the necessary operations to the payload of the message and publishes the results to outbound pipes. Pipes don't route any message or apply any logic, this separation of concerns conferring certain advantages. In particular, it:

- Promotes composability of different pipelines, re-using filters
- Reduces coupling between pipeline components
- Allows filters to be reordered
- Makes it possible to run filters in parallel

The following diagram is a simple representation of the Pipes and Filters architecture:

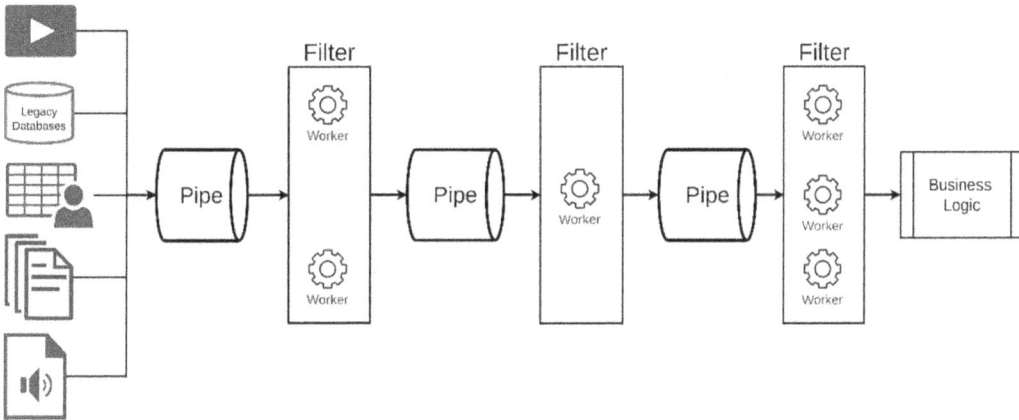

Figure 9.2: A Pipes and Filters architecture example

A couple of points to bear in mind regarding implementation of the Pipes and Filters architecture:

- Workers are great candidates for implementation using asynchronous programming techniques, but be careful about blocking or long-running tasks causing the entire pipeline to suffer a bottleneck on account of a non-released lock over a coroutine.

- Implementations of this architectural style must handle backpressure cases. This means that the performance of the different steps in the data pipeline should be comparable. Otherwise, a fast-processing step might overflow a slow one and break the entire pipeline. This is an especially important consideration when you mix synchronous and asynchronous steps in a single pipeline. The scalability gained from an asynchronous implementation might out-perform a synchronous implementation for a specific step but nevertheless have an overall negative impact at the pipeline level.

Fortunately, there are several great implementations of the Pipes and Filters pattern in Python. In the next section we'll use a library to handle local pipelines executed in a single machine with asynchronous steps.

Working with data pipelines

To work with **asynchronous data pipelines**, we are going to use one of the many open-source libraries that handles steps and orchestration behind the scenes. Our main goal is not to provide custom implementations of the filter-pipe architecture but rather to use it to demonstrate how asynchronous programming can be applied to some steps even though the whole business case might require a combination of both synchronous and asynchronous solutions.

A suitable use case for asynchronous data pipelines

In our case, we want to find the word that has the largest number of related words in any language; to do so we must process a **Parquet file** that contains a structured, comprehensive, multilingual public etymology dataset, etymology being the study of the origin and historical development of words. For example, the word *algorithm* is derived from words in four languages (Middle English, Anglo-Norman, Medieval Latin and Arabic). The following graph shows you the relationships between the root words:

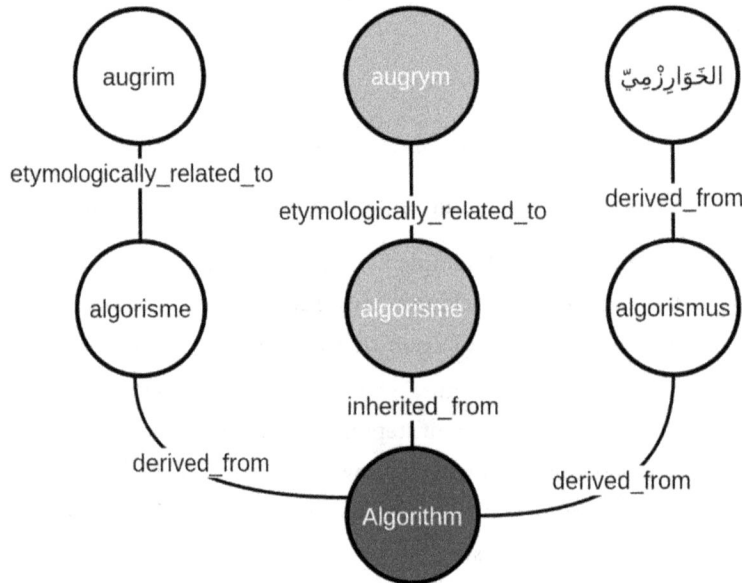

Figure 9.3: The etymology of the word 'algorithm' as an undirected graph

Note about data formats

Data is stored in many formats. Some, like comma-separated values (CSV) or Javascript Object Notation (JSON), keep data in a structured way, and often these text-based formats are combined with separate compression algorithms to save space and speed up transfers (file formats such as zip, bzip2, LZ4, zstd). There are also other file formats for data, such as Parquet, that natively combine both structure and highly efficient compression.

Note that we are going to represent a word's etymology as a **graph**, on the basis that relationships between words are dynamic (many words might have multiple roots or be a combination of several groups of words) and can be typed (they have their own properties). Fortunately, Python provides several libraries and databases for handling graphs, and many of them include algorithms to process our business logic. One of the advantages of the graph as a data structure is that you can join graphs by adding edges between them. For example, *Figure 9.4* shows how four words borrowed from the English 'dictionary' can be linked together to form a larger graph of related words:

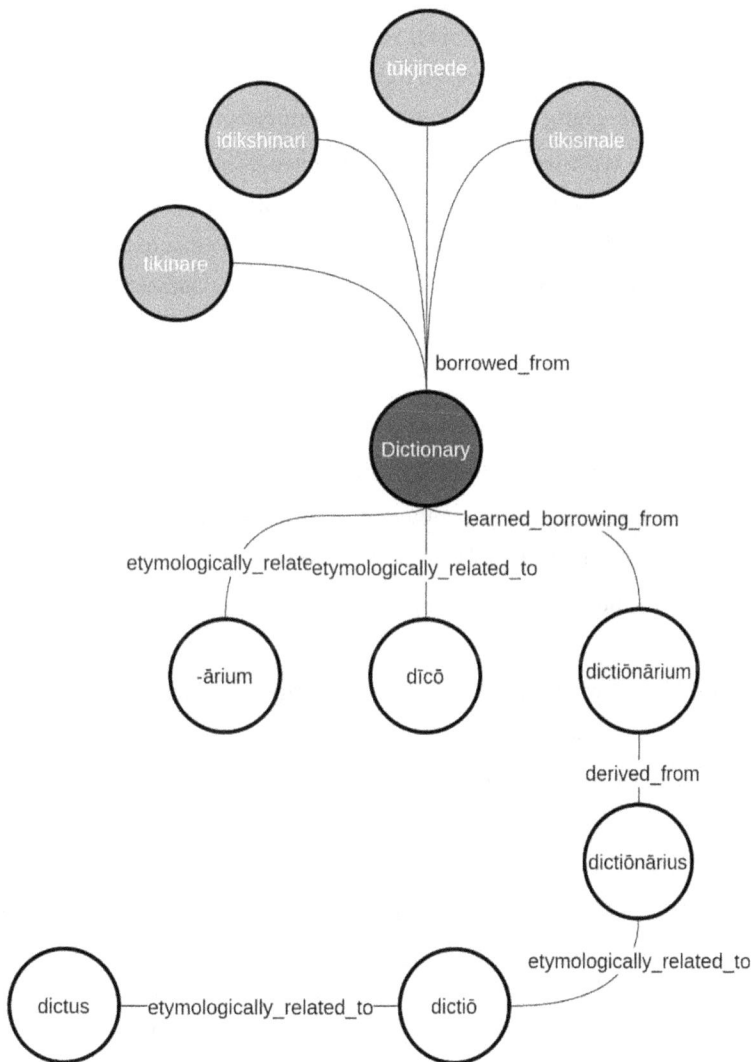

Figure 9.4: Five word-graphs connected as a single larger graph

Using this property of graphs, after processing the entire dataset we can end up with a very large, connected subgraph. Now, to solve our business case our pipeline must then perform several tasks that fit into the ETL categories:

1. **Extraction**: Download the source Parquet file to make it available locally. Usually, this task would involve connecting to a third-party API and transferring numerous files or iterating over several pages of a query resultset from a database. In any case asynchronous I/O operations are a good match for scaling this step.

2. **Extraction**: Given the amount of zipped data in our source file, loading it entirely into memory might not be a good choice. You might instead want to apply a technique we explored in *Chapter 3*: generators. To iterate over the 4+ million rows that we know the file contains we are going to implement a generator to process batches of 50,000 records.

3. **Transformation**: We must implement another generator to group all the records that involve the same source term. This way, several rows of the raw data file will be transformed into a single graph for a particular word. This step holds most of the transformation logic, which is defined by the following data dictionary for the dataset (`https://github.com/droher/etymology-db`) and which provides guidance on how to interpret the data for a single row:

    - **term_id**: A hash of the term and its language.
    - **lang**: The language/dialect of the term.
    - **term**: The term itself. Usually a word, but can also be a prefix or a multi-word expression, hence 'term' instead of a word.
    - **reltype**: The kind of etymological relation being specified (see below for details on each possible value).
    - **related_term_id**: A hash of the related term and its language (useful for assembling relationships across multiple terms).
    - **related_lang**: The language/dialect of the related term. NULL for parent root nodes.
    - **related_term**: The term that is etymologically related to the original entry. NULL for parent root nodes.
    - **position**: Zero-indexed position of the term when the relation is made up of multiple terms (e.g. a compound).

- **group_tag**: Randomly generated ID. Populated only for the root nodes of nested relationships.

- **parent_tag**: If this relation is inside of a nested structure, this will be populated with the group_tag of its immediate parent. NULL otherwise.

- **parent_position**: Zero-indexed position of the relation inside of its nested structure. NULL if not nested.

4. **Load**: We want to load each word-specific graph into a larger graph that contains all the words processed, probably searching for existing nodes and updating their edges as new word-graphs are added. In this way a small graph would be added to a preexisting larger graph.

The following diagram shows Steps 1 to 3 of the pipeline:

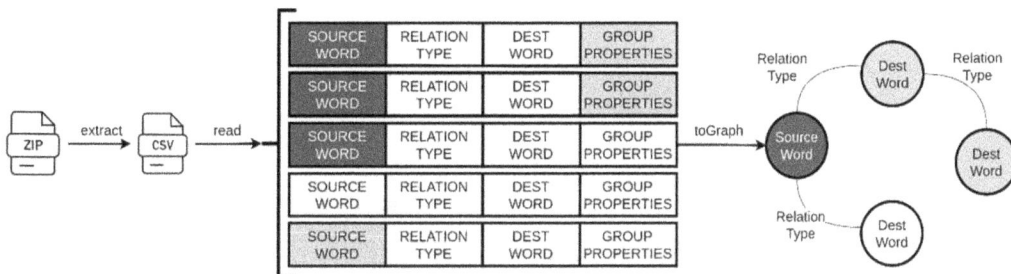

Figure 9.5: A data pipeline candidate for asynchronous implementation

Notice that in the diagram a word-graph is shown sharing the same color source word. Step 3 of the pipeline must detect this series of records and produce a single graph for the source word. The load step can also be divided in a sub-pipeline series of steps, for example:

1. **Extraction**: Return each edge with its associated nodes in the word-graph

2. **Transformation**: Search to see whether the nodes extracted are already in the large destination graph

3. **Load**: Add the nodes not found from the word-graph into the large graph

4. **Load**: Add the edge between the word-graph nodes into the large graph

The following diagram shows the sub-pipeline defined for Step 4 of our data pipeline, using the word-graph for 'dictionary' and adding it to a pre-existing graph that already contains the four words derived from 'dictionary' in languages other than English:

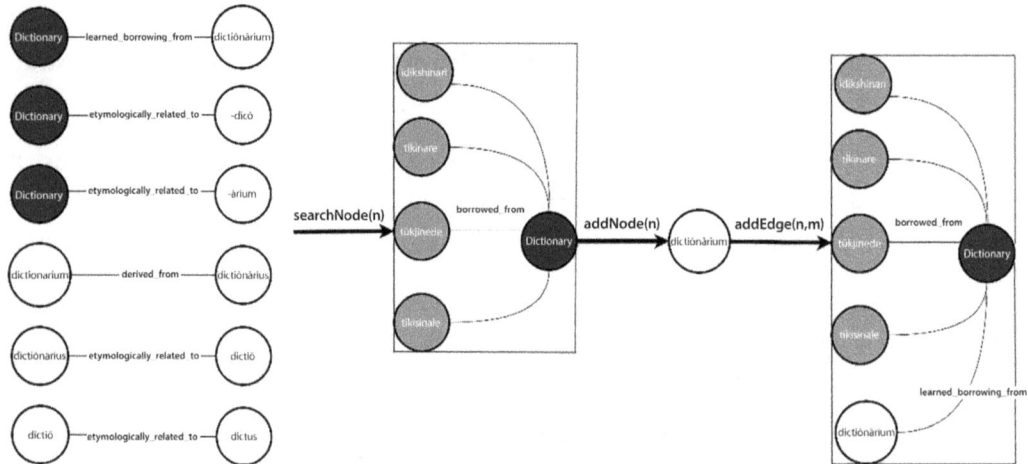

Figure 9.6: A sub-pipeline candidate for asynchronous implementation

Notice that the re-composable nature of data pipelines lets you define alternative ways of processing the data, probably reusing one or more steps (filters) in a different order. Once we have the full graph loaded, we can use one or more of the algorithms in the graph library to implement our business logic, which aims to find the largest subgraph of relations between words.

Asynchronous programming is a good candidate for implementing the steps of this pipeline, since all of them can be modeled as independent concurrent tasks that should perform I/O-bounded tasks for small chunks of data (word graphs). The libraries that handle the data source – zip files containing CSV data – and destination (graph structure) should also support asynchronous I/O operations, to avoid backpressure issues.

Implementing a data pipeline

To orchestrate our data example's pipeline we have chosen the **pyper** (https://pyper-dev. github.io/pyper/) open-source library. This specific implementation has several advantages:

- The steps of a data pipeline can be implemented as coroutines or as synchronous functions
- Data pipelines can mix synchronous and asynchronous steps
- Each step can be executed as a set of async workers, threads or even processes
- Data pipelines can be composed
- Supports nested pipelines

Let's start with the data extraction. Our dataset will be hosted on a public service called **Hugging Face** (`https://huggingface.co/`), which provides hosting capabilities and an open-source Python library to work with hosted datasets. This step is implemented by the following code:

```python
import asyncio
import networkx as nx
from datasets import load_dataset
from typing import AsyncGenerator, Dict, List, Tuple, Any

GLOBAL_GRAPH = nx.Graph()
GLOBAL_GRAPH_LOCK = asyncio.Lock()

def stream_huggingface_etymology_data(hf_dataset):
    dataset_stream = load_dataset(hf_dataset, split="train",
streaming=True)
    for line in dataset_stream:
        yield line
```

The code is fairly simple. The streaming code itself runs synchronously, meaning it processes one item at a time. However, the data pipeline orchestrator (the Pyper library) wraps this synchronous function. This wrapper allows the entire pipeline to run asynchronously by letting other tasks execute while the streaming function is running. The `datasets` library efficiently handles I/O-intensive data downloads internally, making the function appear to yield items asynchronously to pyper. Slow data fetching will cause your pipeline to wait, but it won't fully block the `asyncio` event loop.

The second step is to group records which share the same value in their `term_id` field. Because each record is retrieved as a `dict` we can rely on the generator returned in Step 1 to get the lines to be grouped:

```python
async def group_records_by_term_id(data_stream):
    current_term_id: str | None = None
    current_group_records: List[Dict[str, Any]] = []

    for record in data_stream:
        record_term_id = record['term_id']
        if current_term_id is None:
            current_term_id = record_term_id
```

```
            current_group_records.append(record)
        elif record_term_id == current_term_id:
            current_group_records.append(record)
        else:
            yield (current_term_id, current_group_records)
            current_term_id = record_term_id
            current_group_records = [record]
    if current_group_records:
        yield (current_term_id, current_group_records)
```

This code is a *pre-processing* data step; we are still processing each record in a synchronous way, but are preparing the data by packing all related terms into a single unit that will be passed to Step 3. At this point we can take advantage of one of the characteristics of the Pipes and Filters architecture, which is the ability to test each individual step without having to assemble the whole pipeline. The following code shows a simple test which asserts that the first two terms are streamed and packaged properly using Step 1 and Step 2 implementations:

```
import pytest
import asyncio
from typing import List, Dict, Any

from pipeline_steps import stream_huggingface_etymology_data, group_
records_by_term_id

@pytest.mark.asyncio
async def test_streaming_and_grouping_first_two_term_ids():
    data_stream = stream_huggingface_etymology_data("Nickmancol/mini_
etymology")
    grouped_stream = group_records_by_term_id(data_stream)
    expected_term_ids = [
        "JFwk6_hjU8uJ5NHXEypjtQ",
        "sMQjZAahXbqAUQv3cKiWzg"
    ]
    received_groups = []
    group_count = 0
    async for term_id, records in grouped_stream:
        received_groups.append((term_id, records))
        group_count += 1
```

```
            if gr oup_count >= len(expected_term_ids):
                break
        assert len(received_groups) == len(expected_term_ids)
        assert received_groups[0][0] == expected_term_ids[0]
        assert received_groups[1][0] == expected_term_ids[1]
        assert len(received_groups[0][1]) >= 6
        assert len(received_groups[1][1]) >= 1
```

The test relies on the `pytest-asyncio` plugin (`https://github.com/pytest-dev/pytest-asyncio`) to just assert that each group from the first two terms in the dataset contains the appropriate number of elements.

Step 3 can be decomposed into several parts. The first part encapsulates the logic of how to interpret the relations between terms for each record (see the dataset documentation at `https://github.com/droher/etymology-db` for additional details):

```
def _extract_nodes_and_edges_from_records(records, internal_reltypes):
    nodes_to_add ={}
    edges_to_add = []
    for record in records:
        source_id = record.get('term_id')
        target_id = record.get('related_term_id')
        rel_type = record.get('reltype')

        if source_id:
            current_attrs = nodes_to_add.get(source_id, {})
            current_attrs.update({
            'label': record.get('term', source_id),
            'lang': record.get('lang')
            })
            nodes_to_add[source_id] = {k: v for k, v in current_attrs.
    items() if v is not None}
        if target_id:
            current_attrs = nodes_to_add.get(target_id, {})
            current_attrs.update({
            'label': record.get('related_term', target_id),
            'lang': record.get('related_lang')
            })
            nodes_to_add[target_id] = {k: v for k, v in current_attrs.
```

```
items() if v is not None}
        if source_id and target_id and rel_type and rel_type not in
    internal_reltypes:
            edge_attrs = {
            'reltype': rel_type,
            'position': record.get('position'),
            'group_tag': record.get('group_tag'),
            'parent_tag': record.get('parent_tag'),
            'parent_position': record.get('parent_position')
            }
            cleaned_edge_attrs = {}
            for k, v in edge_attrs.items():
                if v is None:
                    continue
                if isinstance(v, str):
                    stripped_v = v.strip()
                    if stripped_v == '':
                        continue
                    cleaned_edge_attrs[k] = stripped_v
                else:
                    cleaned_edge_attrs[k] = v
            edges_to_add.append((source_id, target_id, cleaned_edge_
    attrs))
        final_nodes = [(node_id, attrs) for node_id, attrs in nodes_to_add.
    items()]
        return final_nodes, edges_to_add
```

The second helper function, _add_main_term_node, identifies and adds the main word (or 'root')
for a group of related words to a subgraph. In our dataset, the root of a word might be not a single
term but a group of related words spread across multiple records.

The function first iterates through the provided records to find the one that represents the main
word of the group. If the main word record is not found, it defaults to the first record in the list.
Once the main word's record is identified, the function adds it as a node to the subgraph. All
other words within the group are discarded, meaning that only the main word acts as the root
for the entire group. This process ensures that a group of related terms is represented by a single,
central node in the graph:

```
def _add_main_term_node(subgraph, group_term_id, records):
    main_term_record = None
    for r in records:
        if r.get('term_id') == group_term_id and not r.get('related_term_
id'):
            main_term_record = r
            break
    if not main_term_record and records:
        main_term_record = records[0]
    if main_term_record:
        subgraph.add_node(group_term_id,
                          label=main_term_record.get('term', group_term_
id),
                          lang=main_term_record.get('lang'))
    else:
        subgraph.add_node(group_term_id, label=group_term_id, lang=None)
```

The last function is the asynchronous Step 3 implementation to process a package of terms, which delegates the actual logic to the previous helper functions:

```
async def create_networkx_subgraph(grouped_data):
    group_term_id, records = grouped_data
    subgraph = nx.DiGraph()
    internal_reltypes = {'group_derived_root', 'group_affix_root',
'internal_grouping_tag'}
    _add_main_term_node(subgraph, group_term_id, records)
    nodes_to_add, edges_to_add = _extract_nodes_and_edges_from_
records(records, internal_reltypes)
    subgraph.add_nodes_from(nodes_to_add)
    subgraph.add_edges_from(edges_to_add)
    yield subgraph
```

In our pipeline, Step 3 (the create_networkx_subgraph function) is designed to run concurrently for multiple batches of terms. This means that while Step 1 (the stream_huggingface_etymology_ data function) continues to ingest records and Step 2 (the group_records_by_term_id function) groups those records into complete collections by term_id, the system won't wait for one subgraph to be fully created before starting work on the next.

Instead, pyper (or any asyncio orchestrator) will take the term groups that Step 2 is yielding and launch separate tasks (though not necessarily in distinct threads or processes) for Step 3 so as to begin building the subgraphs in parallel. This way, while one subgraph is generating, the code can move on to process another group of terms, maximizing CPU resource utilization and reducing total execution time. Each DiGraph that results from this concurrent processing will then be passed to the next step.

Step 4 requires careful handling of a single, shared graph. This is because we can't be sure that the NetworkX library is thread-safe – meaning it isn't designed to handle multiple processes trying to modify the graph at the same time. If multiple processes did try to modify the graph simultaneously it could lead to data corruption or errors. To prevent this, we will add a lock to ensure that only one process can access the graph at a time. The following code shows the implementation of Step 4:

```python
async def merge_into_global_graph(subgraph: nx.DiGraph):
    async with GLOBAL_GRAPH_LOCK:
        GLOBAL_GRAPH.add_nodes_from(subgraph.nodes(data=True))
        GLOBAL_GRAPH.add_edges_from(subgraph.edges(data=True))
```

The GLOBAL_GRAPH_LOCK = asyncio.Lock() is an asynchronous lock (https://docs.python.org/3/library/asyncio-sync.html#asyncio.Lock). When our pipeline runs, it's likely that multiple subgraphs will be generated in interleaved asynchronous tasks. As we said, without a lock, if two tasks tried to add nodes or edges to the GLOBAL_GRAPH simultaneously, it could lead to data corruption or errors. The lock ensures that only one task at a time can execute the code in the with block, guaranteeing that modifications to the graph are atomic and safe.

A better solution is to use a different sink (the destination where data is stored). Instead of using a NetworkX graph as the sink, we can use a graph database built to handle concurrent write/update support. This means the database itself takes on the responsibility of managing simultaneous changes. When we use such a database, the asynchronous lock is effectively delegated, or handed off, to the database's internal system, which automatically handles the synchronization. This makes our code much simpler and more robust, as we no longer need to manage locking manually.

Notice that this is a sink step, which is why the step doesn't return an AsyncGenerator but instead a simple asynchronous coroutine. Now we can assemble the data pipeline to populate the global graph and carry out some analysis over it (source code available at Chapter09/data_pipeline.py):

```
import asyncio
import networkx as nx
from pyper import task
from pipeline_steps import (
stream_huggingface_etymology_data,
group_records_by_term_id,
create_networkx_subgraph,
merge_into_global_graph,
GLOBAL_GRAPH
)
HF_DATASET="Nickmancol/mini_etymology"
async def main():
    pipeline = task(stream_huggingface_etymology_data) | \
        task(group_records_by_term_id, branch=True) | \
        task(create_networkx_subgraph, branch=True) | \
        task(merge_into_global_graph)
    async for _ in pipeline(HF_DATASET):
        pass

if __name__ == "__main__":
    asyncio.run(main())
print("\nPipeline run finished. Summary of the global graph:")
print(f"Nodes: {GLOBAL_GRAPH.number_of_nodes()}")
print(f"Edges: {GLOBAL_GRAPH.number_of_edges()}")
wccs = list(nx.connected_components(GLOBAL_GRAPH))
largest_wcc_nodes = max(wccs, key=len)
S = GLOBAL_GRAPH.subgraph(largest_wcc_nodes)
print(f"Largest subgraph: {S.number_of_nodes()} nodes")
print(f"Largest subgraph: {S.number_of_edges()} edges")
nx.write_gexf(GLOBAL_GRAPH, "etymology_global_graph.gexf")
nx.write_gexf(S, "largest_subgraph.gexf")
```

Running the code creates a Gephi (`https://gephi.org/`) file of the sample dataset (`largest_subgraph.gexf`), which can be rendered as a diagram using one of a range of tools, some of which are available online (`https://lite.gephi.org`). Using a suitable graph visualization algorithm you can generate a depiction of the data that shows the output of the largest connected component, like this:

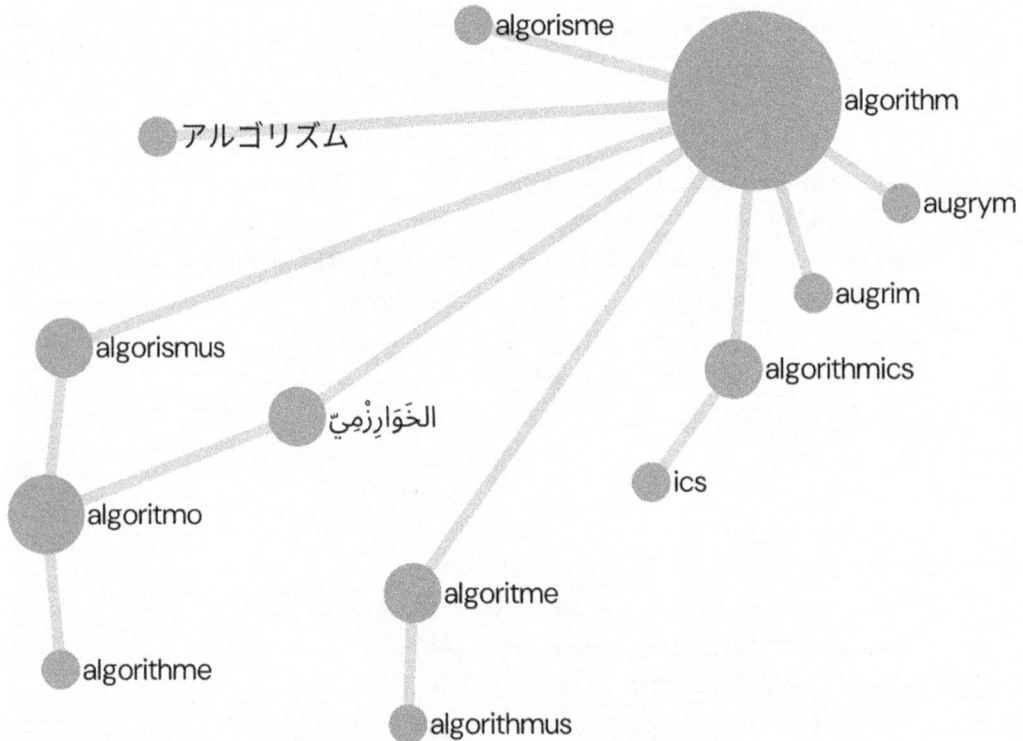

Figure 9.7: The word 'algorithm' as an undirected graph

There are many analyses that can be done with a non-tabular data structure like a graph, and in this case we have focused on a simple analysis performed by a standard algorithm provided by the graph processing library. But you could extend the pipeline to include sub-processing of attributes of nodes, or of different aggregations of nodes, to support more sophisticated use cases.

Scaling data pipelines in cloud environments

The amount of data that can be handled using data pipelines implemented as a single Python script like that presented in the previous sections is usually restricted by the amount of memory (RAM) available. Also, this schema relies completely on a single computer to execute the entire pipeline.

This type of solution puts the emphasis on simplicity – a single python script with the whole data pipeline executed on a single computer – and there may be circumstances where that is to be preferred to an architecture in which execution is distributed.

In many business scenarios where you have big-data kinds of data source, or where there are massive concurrent data streams, you might want to scale even further, and using an architecture featuring a data pipelines orchestrator could be a viable alternative. Several options exist in the market for frameworks and control systems to define, implement, deploy, and observe pipelines implemented in Python.

Each tool/framework has its own specialization, but in general you have a central data pipeline lifecycle manager that schedules individual pipelines to be executed among a swarm of shared independent nodes. This distributed architecture provides great flexibility and scalability, but the hidden costs of managing the underlying infrastructure aren't negligible.

A good strategy is to choose managed services deployed in cloud environments. This gives you the flexibility to scale up as much as you need, but pay only for the resources actually used, according to demand. When selecting a data pipeline orchestration tool the compatibility with multiple runtime environments is one criterion. Other aspects to consider include:

- Support for implementing asynchronous steps
- Support for pipeline testing
- Compatibility with multiple data extraction tools
- Data pipeline version management
- Observability and security (authentication and authorization schemas)
- Exception propagation and handling

Be sure to take into account all the explicit and implicit costs of choosing a tool or framework to scale any data pipeline to big-data levels.

Summary

In this chapter we've investigated an interesting business case that let us model a solution using a versatile and powerful data structure: graphs. Asynchronous data pipelines were implemented to extract, transform and load a dataset to prepare data for the actual analytic business case we wanted to address. The Pipes and Filters architectural pattern lets us take advantage of asynchronous programming workers for several steps of our data pipeline. The segregation of data preparation and business logic is a feature of several architectures, although the asynchronous data pipeline library we used to implement our solution has one clear and explicit limitation: it runs data pipelines on a single machine.

To scale up to big-data use cases, similar techniques are used, but instead of having a local or-chestrator library we might want to use systems capable of distributing pipeline steps across several machines or applying multiprocessing to some of the steps in a pipeline. But the point to emphasize is that asynchronous implementations of data pipelines can handle considerable amounts of data without the hassle of managing distributed or cloud infrastructure.

In the next chapter, more sophisticated use cases for asynchronous programming tasks will be presented as we move from Python scripts to a more comprehensive execution runtime using computational notebooks. Many of the use cases for these are related to data pipelines, data explo-ration, and business intelligence. How to use asynchronous programming in such environments will be the chapter's main focus.

10

Asynchronous Computing with Notebooks

Python's advantages as a programming language include a fast development cycle based on rapid feedback for the developer. This is especially the case when developing scripts and short programs using the REPL (Read-Eval-Print-Loop) style of implementation. Producing more sophisticated products that include elements of hypertext (data, images, links, models, etc.) is facilitated by interactive **computational notebooks**.

We now explore how the paradigm of **interactive computing** that computational notebooks foster is compatible with asynchronous programming, and learn how interactive computing benefits from non-blocking asynchronous operations. Applications for which this combination of tools is appropriate include the simulation of complex processes, data access and analysis, user interfaces and interactive charts, and more.

In this final chapter we'll be covering these topics:

- Interactive computing concepts
- Simulating complexity with asynchronous programming
- Designing user interfaces in notebooks
- Stabilizing simulations with asynchronous programming

Technical requirements

We will be using a variety of external packages besides the standard Python library:

- *HADES*, a framework for creating simulations in Python (`https://ki-oss.github.io/hades/`)
- *Solara*, a library that lets you use and build data-focused web apps (`https://solara.dev`)
- *Dask*, a library for parallel and distributed computing (`https://www.dask.org/`)

As usual the source code is available in the relevant chapter folder of the Github repo (`https://github.com/PacktPublishing/Asynchronous-Programming-in-Python/tree/main/Chapter10`).

In addition, for our simulation example we are going to rely on a **large language model (LLM)** to take some decisions. You can use a container manager like Docker to run local models through **Ollama** (`https://ollama.com/blog/ollama-is-now-available-as-an-official-docker-image`) – a specific script is included in the chapter folder to run Ollama with or without GPU support – or use an external provider with minor code changes. Remember to generate a virtual environment exclusively for the chapter, so that the additional packages do not interfere with other requirements:

```
$ python3 -m venv .env
$ pip install -r requirements.txt
```

Understanding interactive computing

The concept of literate programming was first proposed in the 1980s by the famous programmer Donald Knuth, the idea being that a program should be written in such a way that the thinking behind it is explained through natural language, with the actual code of the program interspersed throughout the explanation. The objective is that the programmer expresses the intentions and mental model/flow through the explanations, and the realizations of those intentions are readable as code and yield instant results – important for shortening the feedback cycle. In principle this could even involve combining multiple programming languages within the same session.

This paradigm has been implemented in the form of specialized programming languages, as well as through simplifications such as keeping documentation close to the code (check Python's Docstring conventions as standardized in PEP-257 – `https://peps.python.org/pep-0257/`). However, the most successful implementation of the literate programming paradigm is the computational notebook, which uses the metaphor of paper blocs for note-taking (i.e. notebooks) to define interactive computational environments in which you can express your thoughts and realize them through code.

Python's characteristics make it an excellent choice for implementing computational notebooks. The Jupyter project (`https://jupyter.org`) created an open specification to combine editors with runtime environments (kernels) that are programming-language agnostic. This specification was initially implemented to support Python, but you can now find computational notebooks offering support for kernels in a variety of languages including Julia, SQL, Kotlin and Rust.

For the rest of this chapter, when we say notebook we mean the **Jupyter Notebook** application used to author and edit notebook files (.ipynb files). To start the integrated editor and execution environment, start the virtual environment and then run JupyterLab (a feature-rich application and editing environment for notebook creation and use):

```
$ source .env/bin/activate
$ jupyter lab
```

Now you can navigate to the local JupyterLab editor by pointing your browser to `http://localhost:8888/lab`. In the left-hand panel a series of tools, including file navigation and extensions to the editor, are shown, and if you open the `async_trust_simulation.ipynb` file you will see that it combines HTML and Python code in a sequence. The HTML is rendered from **Markdown** (a markup language you can use to format document elements using plain text files) and is used to give context to the subsequent pieces of code. The following image gives you a taste of the environment:

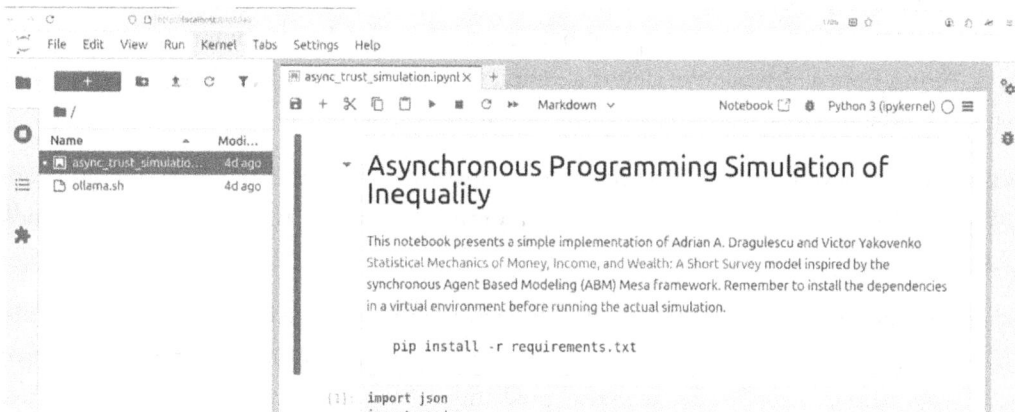

Figure 10.1: JupyterLab editor

The unit of execution in a notebook is a **cell** – the editor highlights the current cell with a vertical bar on the left-hand side, as seen in the previous image – and the execution of cells occurs in a cascade in which later cells have access to previous cells' results and variables.

The JupyterLab editor is not the only one that can handle the *ipynb* standard: almost any modern Integrated Development Environment (IDE) includes support for notebooks, and some popular implementations are free to use online, such as Marimo (`https://molab.marimo.io/notebooks`), Binder (`https://mybinder.org/`), and Google Collab (`https://colab.research.google.com/`). Although our sample notebook is compatible with those environments, you must update a small function to adapt the local dependency on a large language model to using a third-party service. The context and code of our sample will be explained in detail in the next section.

Simulating complexity with asynchronous programming

Simulations are a powerful, but underrated, tool for making informed decisions. A simulation is a controlled scenario in which you model a system that is difficult to frame completely, mentally or analytically. Simulations try to replicate as much as possible the original system, adding some restrictions or conditions to let you explore model outcomes or validate hypotheses in a systematic, controlled and simplified way.

Systems can be classified based on their complexity, although the concept of complexity itself is rather difficult to define. You can associate the idea of complexity with quantitative measurements of some kind, for example information (following Claude Shannon's information theory), with bifurcations and chaos (the number of possible ways in which a system can behave given a set of conditions), or with a definition closer to the theoretical model of computation introduced by A. M. Turing, from which point of view the complexity of a system can be defined in terms of the length of the shortest algorithm capable of generating a model of the system.

A common framework used to classify the complexity of a system is the Cynefin framework (`https://thecynefin.co/about-us/about-cynefin-framework/`), which describes four kinds of system:

- **Simple systems**: In simple systems you have full knowledge of the input and possible outputs of the system; simulations don't add much value beyond automating repetitive operations or confirming analytical predictions. For example, you can simulate the roll of a pair of dice thousands of times to determine what the probability distribution of the sum of outcomes is.

- **Complicated systems**: In this category are systems that have several possible outcomes, with the uncertainty low even if there are multiple outputs or if those outputs occur with different probabilities. This category includes systems like accounting or tax calculation systems that contain a large number of sometimes inconsistent rules that must be followed to obtain a result.

- **Complex systems**: In complex systems there is a lot of uncertainty, which relates to the number things that you are unaware are unknown. For example, transportation is a series of interactions in which as a driver you have a very limited amount of information, in that there are many things you are unaware of, such as aspects of the environment and other drivers' situations. Decisions can have a direct and profound impact on your own behavior and/or that of the entire system.

- **Chaotic systems**: Chaos comes from a lack of order, and in chaotic systems the outcomes of a system look counterintuitive, unpredictable or completely random. This type of system usually presents non-linear dynamics that are highly difficult to model. Weather patterns, neural activity and the movement of billiard balls on an oval table are all examples of chaotic systems.

Asynchronous programming is useful for simulating complex and chaotic systems, given that interactions may occur non-deterministically. In some cases we can assume that our model is composed of externalities that can be non-blocking for the entire system to work. In the following section we are going to model a complex system that involves external components with probabilistic outcomes.

Simulating income inequality

Inequality is a measure of the level of concentration of a resource in a population, and that resource can be income, wealth, opportunity, or any other good or service. The United Nations Sustainable Development Goals 2025 report (available at `https://unstats.un.org/sdgs/report/2025/`) includes figures about the evolution of inequality around the globe, citing the reduction of inequality as one of 17 goals to achieve a better and more sustainable future for all.

It is difficult to create a model to explain how inequality arises in a population, there being many variables that could affect the model in a significant way. Fortunately, however, you can reduce the problem space and create a simulation to estimate to some extent the conditions in which inequality grows or is reduced. We are going to reproduce the Boltzmann Wealth Model, in which a set of agents exchange units of their wealth with other random agents in the population.

The rules of this exchange will be known as a *business*, in which each pair of agents (agent A and agent B) invest the same amount of wealth (one unit) and the result of the *business* depends on a simple calculation based on the strategy of each agent. The calculation is shown in the following table:

If agent A ...	... and agent B ...	Result for A	Result for B
COOPERATES	COOPERATES	2 units	2 units
COOPERATES	CHEATS	-1 units	3 units
CHEATS	COOPERATES	3 units	-1 units
CHEATS	CHEATS	-1 units	-1 units

You might recognize this as an adaptation of the famous prisoner's dilemma (`https://en.wikipedia.org/wiki/Prisoner%27s_dilemma`), a problem in which it is assumed that each agent is rational. That is a strong assumption, and there has been some research on the subject; for example, check out the paper *Are We All Predictably Irrational? An Experimental Analysis* available at `https://link.springer.com/article/10.1007/s11109-019-09579-0`. To model this possible rationality, we are going to delegate the decision of whether to cooperate or cheat in each business to a large language model (LLM), giving it information about the context of the business on each iteration.

To simulate scenarios involving this system we are going to employ a technique called **agent-based modeling (ABM)** and a framework called **HADES** (HADES Asynchronous Discrete-Event Simulation), which provides an engine for executing the simulation in a discrete way. Each timestep of the simulation is queued (in our case we will have one step for each quarter of a year), and events associated with that timestep will be broadcast asynchronously to each agent. Agents execute their actions, and finally the engine checks whether any steps/events remain in the queue. If there are not, the engine ends the simulation. The following diagram shows the simulation flow:

Figure 10.2: HADES asynchronous simulation engine

Our task is to model the system's behavior through the reactions of agents to the timestep/events as they are notified. To do so we are defining two types of agent: *Citizen* agents, which negotiate (do business with other agents) each quarter (a representation of a timestep), and a *Gini Calculator* agent which will be used to measure yearly, in model terms, the Gini coefficient of the population as an indicator of the level of inequality.

To sanity-check the results of our simulation – Gini coefficient per year – we will compare them with actual country data available at *Our World in Data* (`https://ourworldindata.org/economic-inequality`). The following diagram shows the cycle and the interactions between agents in our simulation:

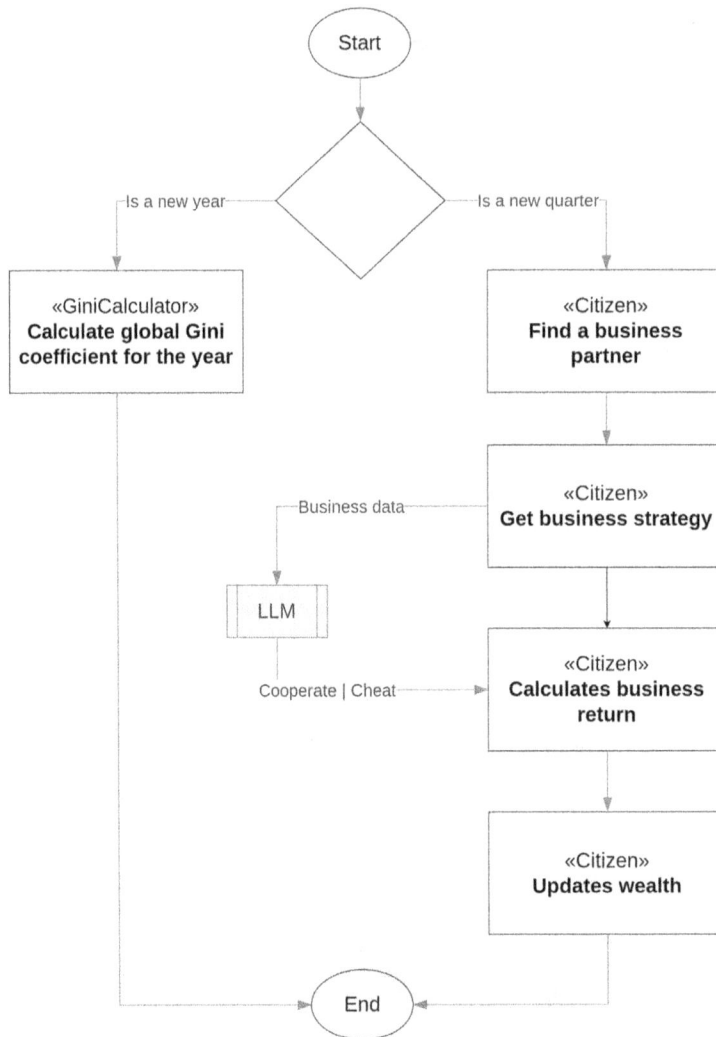

Figure 10.3: Asynchronous tasks occurring on each simulation step

The citizen agent externalizes the decision to choose to cooperate or cheat in each business to an LLM accessed through HTTP as a web service. Note that the order of execution of businesses between citizens is unknown, since those are asynchronous tasks scheduled by the event loop provided by the Jupyter execution environment. The relevant code for the Citizen agent is simple:

```python
class Citizen(Process):
    ...

    async def get_partner(self):
        return self.peers[random.randint(0, len(self.peers)-1)]

    async def prepare_info(self, partner_id:int):
        return {"agent": self.instance_identifier ,"wealth": self.
wealth, "partner_id":partner_id ,"partner_history": self.partner_history.
get(partner_id,[]), "gini": self.gini}

    async def select_tactic(self,partner_instance_id:int):
        business_info = await  self.prepare_info(partner_instance_id)
        tactics = await get_ai_tactic(business_info, self.ai_model)
        business_info.update(tactics)
        self.history.append(business_info)
        return tactics["tactic"]

    async def negotiate(self, t:int, partner):
        result, partner_result = run_business(await self.select_
tactic(partner.instance_identifier) , await partner.select_tactic(self.
instance_identifier))
        self.wealth = self.wealth + result if result > 0 else 0
        partner.wealth = partner.wealth + partner_result if partner_result
> 0 else 0
        ph = self.partner_history.get( partner.instance_identifier, [])
        ph.append(partner_result)
        self.partner_history[partner.instance_identifier] = ph
```

The get_partner method just finds a random partner from the entire population. This could be improved with more sophisticated logic, such as partitioning agents per industry or according to more complicated rules, but for the sake of simplicity we assume that in an egalitarian society any two citizens are willing and able to do business together at any time.

The prepare_info method finds the basic data for the business, including local context (the current agent's wealth and the results of previous negotiations with the selected partner if they exist) and global context (the Gini coefficient calculated for the previous year). Then, the select_tactic method waits for the LLM response given the context and the negotiate method applies the current and partner agent's tactics to calculate the result of the business.

Several helper methods are used in the negotiation:

```python
async def get_random_tactic(business_info:dict):
    return {"tactic":"cooperate" if random.random() > 0.5 else "cheat",
"explanation":"random"}


async def get_ai_tactic( business_info:dict, AI_MODEL:str="qwen3:4b"):
    try:
        completion = await
        #temperature controls the degree of randomness that you might
expect in the LLM responses,
        # 0 means that it should only use the most likely response instead
of exploring other probable alternatives
        AI_client.beta.chat.completions.parse( temperature=0, model=AI_
MODEL, messages=[
                    {"role": "system", "content": problem_context},
                    {"role": "system", "content": json.dumps(business_info)},
                    {"role": "user", "content": "What do you choose? (return
the tactic name (cooperate xor cheat) and then the explanation)"}]
                    , response_format = BizTactic,)
        tactic_response = completion.choices[0].message
        if tactic_response.parsed:
            return {"tactic":tactic_response.parsed.tactic,
"explanation":tactic_response.parsed.explanation}
    except asyncio.CancelledError:
        print(f"Async task cancelled")
    except Exception as e:
        print(f"Error {e}")
    return await get_random_tactic(business_info)


def run_business(tactic1: str, tactic2: str):
    COOPERATE = "cooperate"
    CHEAT = "cheat"
```

```
    t1 = tactic1.lower()
    t2 = tactic2.lower()

    payoff_matrix = {
        (COOPERATE, COOPERATE): (2, 2),  # R: Reward for Mutual
Cooperation
        (COOPERATE, CHEAT): (-1, 3),   # S: Sucker's Payoff, T: Temptation
to Defect
        (CHEAT, COOPERATE): (3, -1),   # T: Temptation to Defect, S:
Sucker's Payoff
        (CHEAT, CHEAT): (-1, -1)      # P: Punishment for Mutual Defection
    }

    return payoff_matrix.get((t1, t2), (0, 0))
```

In our local setup the get_ai_tactic function accepts different values for the LLM model used to obtain a decision, using OpenAI's official API client (https://github.com/openai/openai-python) to wrap the calls to a local Ollama (https://ollama.com/) server. This is a common way to run local AI models. If you want to use a different model provider you just have to modify this function. In case of timeout or cancellation of the async LLM client request task we rely on simple coin toss tactic selection with the get_random_tactic function.

How can we run this simulation? We exploit another interesting capability of notebooks: the ability to run and render non-blocking graphical user interfaces.

Designing user interfaces in notebooks

While REPL environments offer quick feedback, the user experience derived from text-based user interfaces imposes some constraints. Another benefit of interactive notebooks is that the community and the market have developed libraries that extend the rendering capabilities to support not only code with kernels, or static hypertext through markup languages, but also charts and interactive non-blocking user interfaces.

We set up and run our simulation by creating a class to initialize the HADES engine with the agents and context variables we desire for our simulation. This class also holds the information we will later use to analyze the results. The code is straightforward:

```
class SimRunner:
    def init(self, num_agents: int, num_years: int, ai_model:str =
"qwen3.4b"):
```

```
        self.total_agents = num_agents
        self.years = num_years
        self.ai_model = ai_model
        self.hades = Hades()
        self.initialize()


    def initialize(self):
        self.agents = [Citizen(i, self.ai_model) for i in range(self.
total_agents)]
        for agent in self.agents:
            self.hades.register_process(agent)
            agent.peers = [a for a in self.agents if a.instance_identifier
!= agent.instance_identifier]
            self.gini_calculator = GiniCalculator(self.agents)
            self.hades.register_process( self.gini_calculator)
            self.hades.register_process( YearStartScheduler(2025, self.
years))
            self.hades.register_process( QuarterStartScheduler())

    @property
    def wealths(self):
        return self.gini_calculator.all_wealth

    @property
    def gini(self):
        return self.gini_calculator.all_gini

    @property
    def log_df(self):
        return pd.DataFrame([item for sublist in [a.history for a in self.
agents] for item in sublist])
```

The HADES engine provides two schedulers, YearStartScheduler and QuarterStartScheduler, which will generate an event for each new timestep simulated up to the maximum number of years configured.

Now to create a user interface we use a framework called **Solara** (`https://solara.dev/`) that extends Jupyter's native widget render capabilities (check the *ipywidgets* project at `https://ipywidgets.readthedocs.io/en/stable/`) to include non-blocking reactive capabilities. The Solara project defines user interfaces through pages that contain widgets for visual structure, input of data or rendering information. Combining some elements we can easily get a working user interface rendered as the output of a notebook cell:

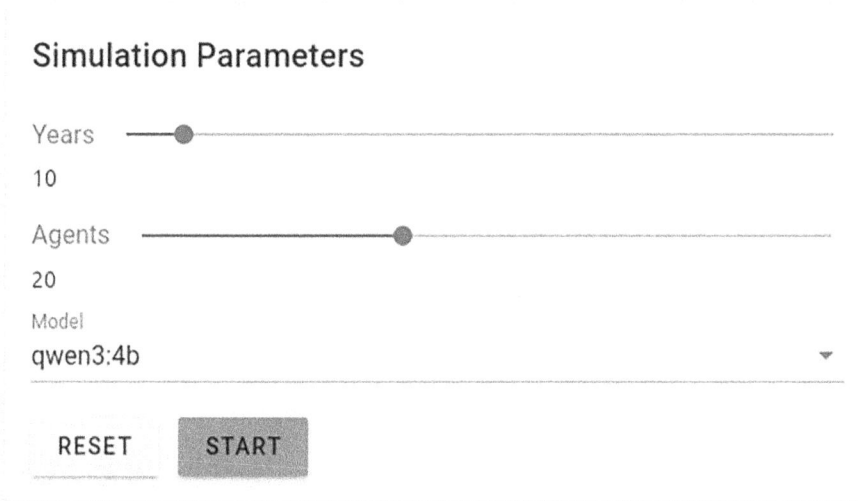

Simulation Parameters

Years ———●——————————————————————
10

Agents ——————————————●————————————
20

Model
qwen3:4b ▾

RESET　　START

Figure 10.4: User interface to control simulation execution

Solara also provides the `reactive` class, which can be used to handle the states of variables in a simple manner. In our case we set up three environment-controlling variables: years that will be simulated, the number of agents that will be interacting, and the LLM that will be used to make the citizen's tactical decision. The following code shows how the UI is built and the `SimRunner` class is used to execute the simulation using the parameters configured through the UI:

```
@solara.lab.task
async def run_sim():
    runner = SimRunner(total_agents.value, years.value, model.value)
    await runner.hades.run()
    return runner


@solara.component
def Page():
    with solara.Columns([1, 2]):
```

```
        with solara.Card(title="Simulation Parameters", margin=1):
            solara.SliderInt("Years", value=years, min=2, max=100)
            solara.Markdown(f"{years.value}")
            solara.SliderInt("Agents", value=total_agents, min=2, max=50)
            solara.Markdown(f"{total_agents.value}")
            solara.Select(label="Model", value=model, values=models)
            with solara.Row():
                solara.Button("Reset", on_click=reset_vals)
                solara.Button("Start", color="green", on_click=run_sim)

    with solara.Card(margin=1):
        solara.ProgressLinear(run_sim.pending)
        if run_sim.finished:
            df = run_sim.value
            solara.FigureMatplotlib(get_plots(runner))
        elif run_sim.not_called:
            solara.Text("Click the START button to simulate, then, wait
for it")
        elif run_sim.cancelled:
            solara.Text("Cancelled the fetch")
        elif run_sim.error:
            solara.Error(str(run_sim.exception))

Page()
```

The **start** button runs the run_sim coroutine as a Solara task, instead of as a normal asyncio task. This Solara Task (https://solara.dev/documentation/components/lab/task) object is used by the framework to execute the coroutine in a separate thread, thereby avoiding blocking the UI while long-term functions or coroutines like our simulation are executing.

In our case, augmenting the number of agents and/or years might increase the total execution time, because even if we have set up requests to the external LLM service in an asynchronous way we cannot guarantee the levels of service or response times from that service. In this case asynchronous programming allows us to execute more business concurrently but doesn't reduce the time required to execute an individual negotiation between two agents.

Important note

Before running the simulation in your Jupyter notebook environment, make sure you start the local Ollama server with the LLMs pulled in advance. A companion shell script (`Chapter 10/ollama.sh`) to run Ollama server from Docker is available along with the sample source code for this chapter, downloadable from the GitHub repo.

The script will download the latest Ollama Docker image and a set of models used in the code for comparison purposes. You can run the script from the terminal with the following command:

```
$ cd Chapter\ 10/
$ ./ollama.sh
```

Once the script finishes it will show a confirmation message. You can modify the script to change the LLMs used or even hook to LLM APIs instead of running locally.

Once you hit the **start** button, the engine will execute the simulation, and each agent will asynchronously apply its behavior rules. The global cumulative consequences are difficult to predict, given that the actual decision maker is a probabilistic black box (the LLM) rather than a population of humans! We can check the results of the simulation by examining two charts: the evolution of the global Gini coefficient over time and the agent's aggregated wealth distribution:

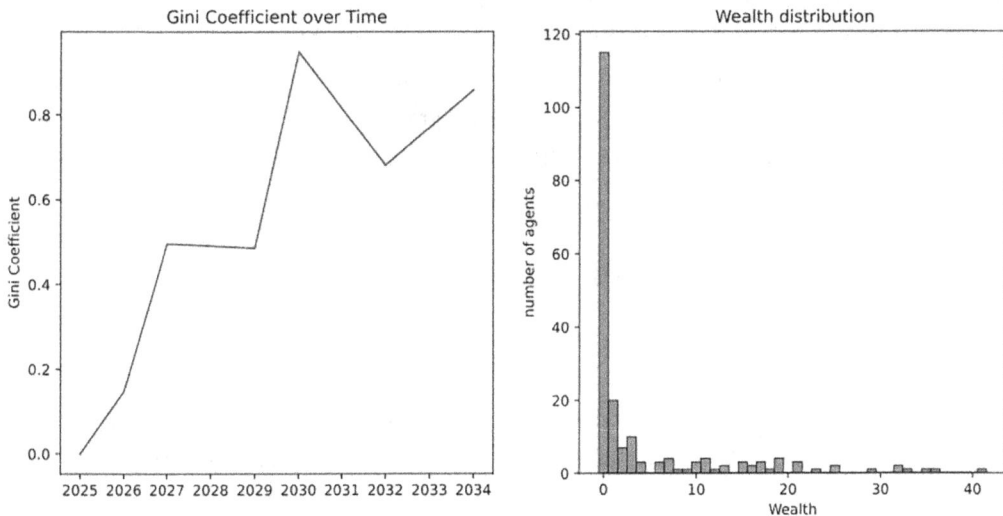

Figure 10.5: Simulation global results

The analysis of these results is beyond the scope of this chapter, but it is easy to see that inequality emerges even if each agent takes it into account (remember that the level of inequality expressed as a Gini coefficient is passed to the LLMs as part of the global context of each business) before making their own decisions. It's also interesting to plot two companion statistics – the percentage of situations in which the LLM decides to cheat or cooperate, and the percentage of decisions that were not random – that illustrate the behavior of the agents:

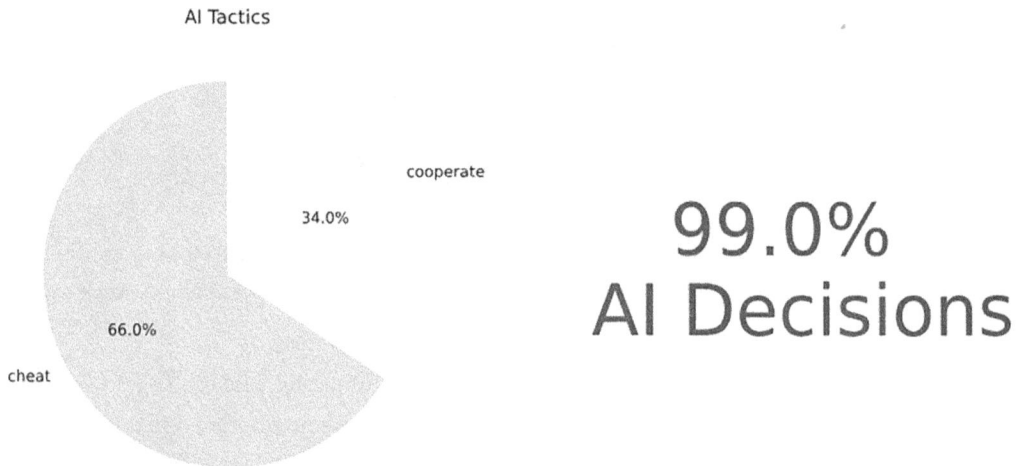

AI Tactics

cooperate

34.0%

99.0%
AI Decisions

66.0%

cheat

Figure 10.6: Simulation global results

Since 99% of the business decisions were taken by LLMs, and the majority (66%) of those decisions were to use the 'cheat' tactic instead of the cooperative approach, it is interesting to ask why those LLMs prefer individual returns to global welfare. That question is also beyond the scope of this book. Nevertheless, we can use asynchronous programming to try to corroborate our initial simulated results, introducing scenarios with minimal variations in the initial conditions to check whether the model results are stable or over-sensitive.

Stabilizing simulations with asynchronous programming

There are many ways to check whether a simulation shows reasonable results, besides the code-smell tests and the verification of reasonable defaults in assumptions (for example the rationality of the agents is a strong assumption in models). You can run the same scenario several times or vary a single parameter to check whether the results show too much variation on each run or change. In this task you can also employ the asynchronous programming techniques discussed previously to launch several asyncio tasks simultaneously, running the same model with slight differences.

In our case we choose to keep the scenarios with 20 agents making business for 10 years (40 quarters), but changing for each execution the LLM that will make the cooperate or cheat decision:

```
agents = 20
years = 10
models = ["cogito:8b","gemma3n:e4b","granite3.3:8b","qwen3:4b"]
runners = [SimRunner(agents, years, m) for m in models]
await asyncio.gather(*[r.hades.run() for r in runners])
line_styles = ['-', '--', '-.', ':']
colors = ['black', 'black']
fig = plt.figure()
fig.set_figwidth(12)
for i, r in enumerate(runners):
    sns.lineplot(r.gini, label=r.ai_model, linestyle=line_styles[i %
len(line_styles)], color=colors[i % len(colors)])
plt.ylabel("Gini coefficient")
plt.title("Comparing different AI models")
plt.legend()
plt.show()
```

The code uses the asyncio gather function to schedule and await all executions concurrently. We don't know in which order they will be executed, but once all tasks are completed we can plot the results for comparison:

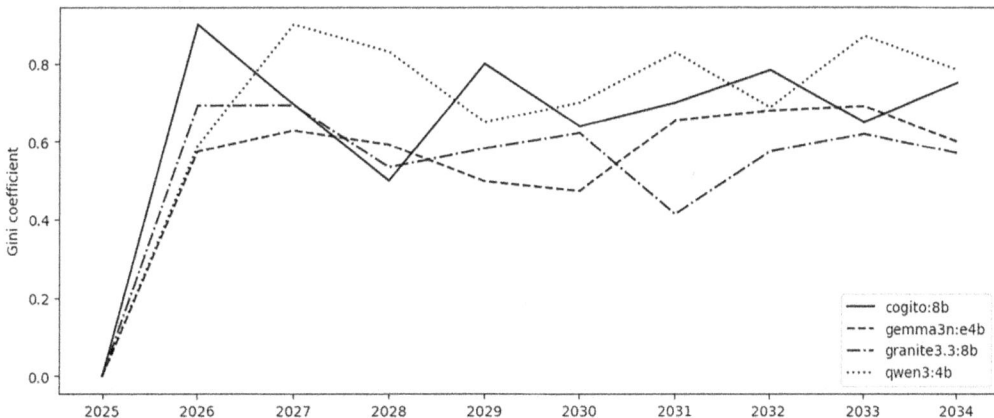

Figure 10.7: Concurrent simulation with different LLMs as parameters

For the sake of completeness let's compare the results for two countries for which inequality data is available over a period of 10 years:

Gini Coefficient 2013-2023

World Bank (2025). Poverty and Inequality Platform – processed by Our World in Data

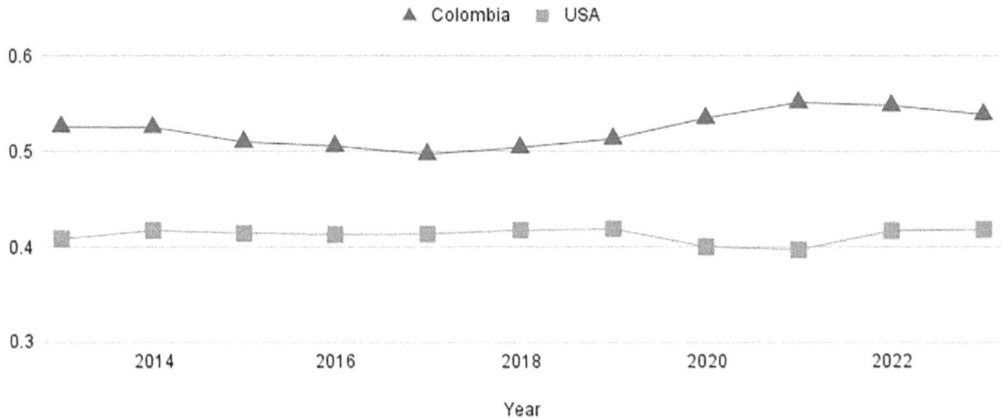

Figure 10.8: Gini coefficient 2013 to 2023, USA and Colombia

It looks like our model is somewhat stable despite the LLM, but certainly more pessimistic about the population's altruism in their decisions.

Summary

And so we've reached the end of our journey. That journey began with a conceptual review of how computers handle multiple operations, and we then walked through the features and incremental improvements made to Python to manage concurrent operations: capabilities like multiprocessing, multithreading, generators and coroutines. After that we reviewed some of the main patterns, pitfalls and other considerations to bear in mind when dealing with asynchronous workloads. With those concepts and basic constructs in place, we explored several asynchronous-enabled solutions for different contexts, including web applications and relational and non-relational data access, as well as data pipelines.

In this last chapter we have explored the application of asynchronous programming techniques in an interactive environment that implements the literate programming paradigm – computational notebooks – which has been proposed as a solution to giving context about software intentions.

To illustrate the advantages of asynchronous programming in handling the scalability required to model complex systems we implemented a model to investigate the phenomenon of wealth inequality, relying on external systems in the form of LLMs accessed through non-blocking mechanisms. Finally, we used some of the previously explored concurrent execution techniques to scale simulation execution to multiple scenarios, with minor variations.

Overall, the lesson is clear: asynchronous programming does not guarantee instantaneous performance improvements unless you understand the type of workload you are running. Non-blocking input/output operations are the most susceptible to improvement by asynchronous programming, but there are always tradeoffs to be made, typically in terms of tracing and error handling. Fortunately, the Python ecosystem provides many tools to improve our programming experience and the readability of asynchronous programs – as this chapter has shown.

11

Unlock Your Exclusive Benefits

Your copy of this book includes the following exclusive benefits:

- ☁ Next-gen Packt Reader
- 📄 DRM-free PDF/ePub downloads

Follow the guide below to unlock them. The process takes only a few minutes and needs to be completed once.

Unlock this Book's Free Benefits in 3 Easy Steps

Step 1

Keep your purchase invoice ready for *Step 3*. If you have a physical copy, scan it using your phone and save it as a PDF, JPG, or PNG.

For more help on finding your invoice, visit https://www.packtpub.com/unlock-benefits/help.

> **Note:** If you bought this book directly from Packt, no invoice is required. After *Step 2*, you can access your exclusive content right away.

Step 2

Scan the QR code or go to `packtpub.com/unlock`.

On the page that opens (similar to *Figure 11.1* on desktop), search for this book by name and select the correct edition.

Figure 11.1: Packt unlock landing page on desktop

Step 3

After selecting your book, sign in to your Packt account or create one for free. Then upload your invoice (PDF, PNG, or JPG, up to 10 MB). Follow the on-screen instructions to finish the process.

Need help?

If you get stuck and need help, visit `https://www.packtpub.com/unlock-benefits/help` for a detailed FAQ on how to find your invoices and more. This QR code will take you to the help page.

Note: If you are still facing issues, reach out to `customercare@packt.com`.

‹packt›

packtpub.com

Subscribe to our online digital library for full access to over 7,000 books and videos, as well as industry-leading tools to help you plan your personal development and advance your career. For more information, please visit our website.

Why subscribe?

- Spend less time learning and more time coding with practical eBooks and Videos from over 4,000 industry professionals
- Improve your learning with Skill Plans built especially for you
- Get a free eBook or video every month
- Fully searchable for easy access to vital information
- Copy and paste, print, and bookmark content

At www.packtpub.com, you can also read a collection of free technical articles, sign up for a range of free newsletters, and receive exclusive discounts and offers on Packt books and eBooks.

Other Books You May Enjoy

If you enjoyed this book, you may be interested in these other books by Packt:

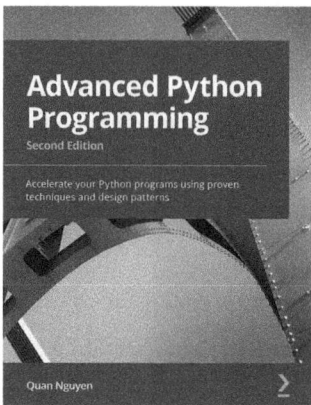

Advanced Python Programming

Quan Nguyen

ISBN: 9781801814010

- Write efficient numerical code with NumPy, pandas, and Xarray
- Use Cython and Numba to achieve native performance
- Find bottlenecks in your Python code using profilers
- Optimize your machine learning models with JAX
- Implement multithreaded, multiprocessing, and asynchronous programs
- Solve common problems in concurrent programming, such as deadlocks
- Tackle architecture challenges with design patterns

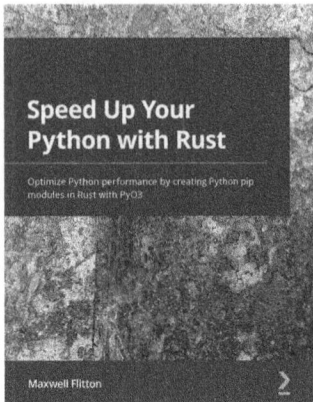

Speed Up Your Python with Rust

Maxwell Flitton

ISBN: 9781801811446

- Explore the quirks of the Rust programming language that a Python developer needs to understand to code in Rust
- Understand the trade-offs for multiprocessing and thread safety to write concurrent code
- Build and manage a software project with cargo and crates
- Fuse Rust code with Python so that Python can import and run Rust code
- Deploy a Python Flask application in Docker that utilizes a private Rust pip module
- Inspect and create your own Python objects in Rust

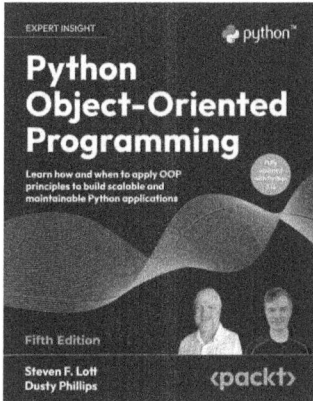

Python Object-Oriented Programming

Steven F. Lott, Dusty Phillips

ISBN: 9781836642596

- Write Python classes and implement object behaviors
- Apply inheritance, polymorphism, and composition
- Understand when to use OOP—and when not to
- Use type hints and perform static and runtime checks
- Explore common and advanced design patterns in Python
- Write unit and integration tests with unittest and pytest
- Implement concurrency with asyncio, futures, and threads
- Refactor procedural code into well-designed OOP structures

Packt is searching for authors like you

If you're interested in becoming an author for Packt, please visit `authors.packt.com` and apply today. We have worked with thousands of developers and tech professionals, just like you, to help them share their insight with the global tech community. You can make a general application, apply for a specific hot topic that we are recruiting an author for, or submit your own idea.

Share your thoughts

Now you've finished *Asynchronous Programming in Python*, we'd love to hear your thoughts! Scan the QR code below to go straight to the Amazon review page for this book and share your feedback or leave a review on the site that you purchased it from.

`https://packt.link/r/1836646615`

Your review is important to us and the tech community and will help us make sure we're delivering excellent quality content.

Index